Cinnamongirl Presents

I Am the Dream

Voices of a New Generation

Cinnamongirl Presents

I Am the Dream
Voices of a New Generation

Edited by
Mina Witteman

cinnamongirl

BAY AREA BOOK FESTIVAL

Copyright © 2022 by Cinnamongirl, Inc. and the respective authors

Compilation Copyright © by Mina Witteman

All rights reserved. No part of this publication may be reproduced, stored in a retrieval system, or transmitted in any form or by any means, electronic, mechanical, photocopying, recording, or otherwise, without the prior permission of both the copyright owner of the story and the above publisher of this book.
For information address Cinnamongirl, Inc.,
PO Box 27411, Oakland, CA 94602.

www.cinnamongirl.org

Except for the memoir pieces, these are works of fiction. All characters, organizations, and events portrayed in this anthology are either products of the author's imagination or are used fictitiously.

ISBN (PB): 978-1-0880-3193-3
ISBN (E): 978-1-0880-3194-0

Typeset by Roland Pilcz
Cover design by Innosanto Nagara and Roland Pilcz
Cover image by Laila Butcher

Printed and bound in the United States of America by IngramSpark

> Until the lion learns to write,
> every story will glorify the hunter.
> - *African Proverb*

Contents

I Am the Dream by Naujda Davis-Van Hook	9
Foreword by Renée Richard	11
Blacker Than You by Aisha Renée Diop	18
In My Court by Erikah Sanders	34
Killer Kids by Jolie Wilson	52
Fighting For Change by Laila Butcher	69
Why Was It Me? by Rowan Feldman	72
The Truth Behind a Mask by Giselle Caban	90
Black Blood - 5 Poems by Naujda Davis-Van Hook	113
The Art of a Black Girl - 5 Poems by Clover Waddell	118
Cat Tale by Alanna Williams	127
The Clash of Past and Present by Chariot Waddell	146
The Eye of the Stone by Jennifer Leon	163
The Dragon Chronicles by Kaya Bullard	183
Blood in the Snow by Mackenzie Bell	207
The Magic of Ms. Magissa by Mariah McCoy	224
Acknowledgments	241
Author Biographies	243
About Cinnamongirl	248

I AM THE DREAM
by Naujda Davis-Van Hook, Age 12

I am the dream

The shooting star you wish upon

That strides upon the abundant sky

The sky full of the stars that you reach for

I am the dream

I am hope

Love

Anger

Happiness

Sadness

You are a new star in creation

You are now a star in the sky

The sky full of the stars that you now hold in your hand

And as long as you fulfill your duty

To your heart,

Your dream will exist forever and ever

We are the dream

Foreword
by Renée Richard

In the spring of 2003, I had three fun and very busy children: two boys, Julien, 8, and Josh, 6, and a girl, Jayla, age 4. All three attended a local private Montessori school just a few blocks away from our home. Through its international community of teachers and students from cultures all over the world, my children received a rich educational foundation. They were taught multiple languages, read rigorously, and learned about geography, geometry, and the sciences. We were one of the few families of color, and we never felt ostracized. We knew we were an integral part of the school community. Though this was fantastic, I knew the world wasn't this accepting and it was important for my children to have diverse friends of color too. The boys played sports across Oakland neighborhoods, but my little girl was different. I wanted her to have a plethora of girls to play with, some Black, some brown, some of humble means, and some wealthy, and I wanted her to feel beautiful with her curly locks and brown skin.

A girl develops a strong sense of confidence and self-love by learning and acquiring wisdom from mentors who have achieved success. Eventually, she will grow to never question herself or feel the need for validation from the outside world because she knows who she is on the inside. I did not encounter spaces that offered that, a judgment-free environment where girls of color of different backgrounds could be in dialogue and even debate, a place that cultivated a curious mind. I had never experienced such a space before going to college and, around me, I saw girls become disenchanted and disengaged during middle and high school years. If there was to be such a place, I would need to create it: a powerful pipeline of female leaders, a social and intellectual space with people young Black girls could look up to, a sorority of women and girls of color with unique interests and passions. I wanted my little girl to always know her greatness, regardless of her pursuits.

I created Cinnamongirl, Inc., a program for girls of color with self-reliance as its major teaching pillar. I knew that I could take a girl from ordinary circumstances and immerse her in greatness, and the experience and knowledge gained would have the potential to change her entire life-trajectory. She may have already believed she was on a fantastic journey but had not been given the tools to achieve an incredible life. I wanted to create a safe space that would encourage girls to be fearless in their dreams, whatever they might be: a president of a major corporation, a mayor of a big city, a leader of the United Nations, or perhaps the owner of a business.

To create the foundation for this experience, I turned to my brilliant sister-friends and some parents at my children's school. They became my early supporters. Within a few months, I had met with incredibly accomplished women who wanted to pour their knowledge and energy into a young girl's life. With four amazing women, we began spending quality time as a group with eight girls. A few more friends helped me form what has come to be our Cinnamongirl founding board.

Cinnamongirl gained recognition with other Black families because parents and guardians saw that we were one of the only organizations that worked specifically with Black girls building achievement. When the girls saw their mammoth dreams valued, our organization became a sacred space. The girls realized that we were serious about their goals, and they showed up at meetings every week and spent time learning about college life, about non-traditional careers, and about investing. They spent time with mentors visiting museums, science labs, musicals, and poetry slams. Our tagline became "The World is Our Playground."

For over fifteen years, Cinnamongirl has created relationships between our girls and amazing women and men. 98% of the girls have graduated high school and gone on to fantastic colleges and graduate programs. Our mentors accelerated in their careers as well. Many had started out as first or second level managers, and in time, they were promoted to top levels within their firms. The Cinnamongirls' dreams were taking flight and with it we saw phenomenal growth with their mothers too.

But Cinnamongirl as an organization struggled. We were not able to attract donors to support our work the way we needed, and funders passed on our proposals. We realized that Cinnamongirl, as a predominantly Black organization, wasn't valued by white-led organizations. Cash and funding opportunities were not making their way to us. Family foundations didn't know us or understand how dedicated we were. When they did, they were more enamored with the idea of 'saving a kid' than by elevating girls' dreams.

Fast forward to 2017 when my sister and mentor Ms. Deborah Santana asked Cinnamongirl to participate in a reading event of *All the Women in My Family Sing*, a collection of essays she published that were written by women of color about family, love, equality, justice, freedom, body image, identity, racism, and the human condition. After the book presentation, Deborah shared her vision of the need to have more women of color involved in all aspects of the literary industry. She shared some publishing statistics including how Toni Morrison, during her tenure from 1967 to 1983 as an editor at Random House, the largest of the five big publishers, championed many authors of color but was able to see only a dismal 3.3% of the books published by these authors of color. That number nosedived when Ms. Morrison left the company. Of the 512 books published by Random House between 1984 and 1990, only two were written by Black authors. One of them was *Beloved* by Ms. Morrison herself.

I was stunned. I did my own research and learned that just about every major decision maker at the five major publishing houses is white. These houses publish 80% of the books in the US. They make the decisions as to which authors they sign, who receives the promotional monies, and, ultimately, which stories are brought to the US market. No wonder the stories of women of color weren't told. These decision makers were not interested in stories that were seen through a different lens than their own because they couldn't identify with them and could not see that there was a market for these stories. And they weren't prepared to take risks. The only way to get more diverse stories out on the market, Deborah reminded, is to get more diverse people involved in all aspects of publishing. Over time, she was sure, we would see more diverse writers and their stories.

Shortly following Deborah's talk, I began restructuring Cinnamongirl such that we could serve more girls and provide even more in-depth programming. I decided on a cohort model, and the first cohort, Travelgirl, was formed. Traveling to amazing places around the globe had been a dream that I had since Cinnamongirl's inception. Eight girls and four mentors embarked on an incredible adventure to Senegal in June of 2019 to see the "Door of No Return" and the lands where many of our ancestors once lived. Partnered with a Senegalese American school, we met with native girls who had studied abroad and who had traveled the world. Their French and English were so fluent, we couldn't tell which was their first language. The following year, in an amazing partnership with the Commonwealth Club, we traveled with college-aged girls to the South to understand the Civil Rights Movement. We met with a Freedom Rider; a man born on a Greenwood plantation who picked cotton for many years; and one of the best friends of the four innocent girls who were killed in the 16th Street church bombing in Birmingham, Alabama. Our girls came away from this rich learning with dreams for their lives that would never have been conceived were it not for these travels.

But Deborah Santana's words about stories and publishing kept resonating and in 2020 Cinnamongirl launched what I believe to be one of the most important programs we offer young girls: Write Your Story. Write Your Story is a cohort of girls of color, ages twelve and up, compelled to share their thoughts in stories and poems, in fiction and nonfiction. Most stories written today are still not the stories of Black and brown people and not having stories from people of color is like having potatoes for dinner every night. Eventually, you will crave something different and, boy, when you taste jambalaya or enchiladas you may not want another potato for quite some time.

A powerful story can change people. It can make them more empathetic. It allows them to see perspectives they never considered before. A new story creates a larger world of inclusion and understanding. When a person of color is able to fully participate in an artform, a sport, or industry, they will, without a doubt, do things differently because of their unique perspective. Crafting a space for a girl of various backgrounds to write not only helps refine her ability to communicate but gives the world the opportunity to read a story that is layered with different textures and flavors, with new phrases and with words we have never read before. It alters our perspective, our ability to feel, and it elevates us altogether. I will never forget this African proverb shared by Deborah: "Until the lion learns to write, every story will glorify the hunter."

Our Write Your Story program is a rigorous, college-level writing course. Our faculty of award-winning authors of color and professional writers deliver over forty hours of top-notch instruction and coaching to our girls. Our writing space expands the avenues through which girls of color and gender expansive youth share their experiences. It creates a safe haven to explore paths toward healing, ingenuity, and courage.

I hope this program will grow and continue through the ages, as I believe the world is finally waiting with great anticipation for the stories told through a person of color's lens. In the last ten years over half the national book awards for fiction were awarded to authors of color. But that is still fewer than 10 books. I believe that we will see many more programs like Write Your Story and soon there will be more people of color rising in the ranks of publishing, editing, and storytelling.

The Cinnamongirl stories in this anthology, *I Am The Dream*, are as unique as our writers' styles. They are intricate and unpredictable. What I like most is that diversity is artfully woven into each story. My Cinnamongirls do a phenomenal job in capturing the plethora of their emotions, allowing the reader to immerse their whole self in and through the story.

Blacker than You
by Renée Diop, Age 16

I cut the thick, white construction paper into the shape of a heart, watching my dark reflection in the dulled blade of the scissor. I held it up and surveyed my clean work. A perfectly shaped heart, like I'd drawn it from a stencil. I reached over to grab the glue from the bucket at the center of the table when a call came from across the room. It was my teacher, Mrs. Handler. I dropped my work and went to meet her.

"Yes?" I asked, looking up expectantly.

She held up a finger before answering, calling another student to join me. "Riley? Yes, come here."

Riley. Another classmate of mine. Not much to say about Riley. She rarely talked to the other kids, let alone me.

"I'm gonna send you girls to a room." Mrs. Handler bent down to meet me at eye level. She handed me a sticky note with the number to a classroom. "You're going to spend the rest of class there today."

I took the note from her hand and held open the heavy door for Riley. We walked through the poster-plastered corridors in silence, with her always a few meters behind me. I pondered; this could mean one of two things: we'd done something wrong, or we'd done something right. My excitement peaked, remembering being selected for an advanced math class last year, being ushered out of the room to a special group with more challenging problems to work on. It had to be something like that.

I looked back at Riley, with her hands behind her back, looking down at her feet as she walked. I didn't pay her much attention in class, but she was probably good at math.

When we made it to the classroom, the door was held ajar by a worn black stopper, pinched into the fuzzy carpet of the school. A handmade sign, a piece of paper taped to the glass, read *Buddy Club*. Okay... didn't sound very mathematical, but I could be wrong.

A teacher I'd never met and some students I'd recognized from the playground were inside the room, chairs pulled into a circle. Some of them were familiar; they always sat at the same table at lunch off to the side, really quiet. Didn't know a whole lot about them, like Riley. We were made to sit, and the little meeting commenced.

"Hel-*lo* everyone!" the stranger of a teacher said, voice a little too high-pitched. It's not like we were third graders anymore. "For my new faces here, my name is Ms. Gonz*aaa*lez, and this is the Buddy Club!" She began to clap, so we followed, patting our hands slowly. "This is a chill-ax club to just make friends and just have fun!"

So, this is where things clicked into place. The quiet kids, a club to make friends. Sure, whatever. But why was *I* there?

My fourth-grade teacher had good intentions, and in hindsight, I thank her for putting me in that club. Nothing came of it in terms of making friends, because I quit after two meetings, thinking it was a waste of time. Though, it did serve as a wake-up call. Sure, I wasn't super shy like the other kids, but definitely I wasn't put there for *no* reason.

But I really wasn't *that* kid. The one that eats their lunch in the bathroom stall and sits in the back of the class with their head down. Instead, I was that kid whose hand shot up when the teacher asked for a volunteer. I was that kid who always ran to be first in line, to lead the class through the halls with my head held high. I was that kid who did most of the work on the group project, organizing tasks for the others.

And even outside of my clear ambitions for leadership, I *was* social. I approached people at recess, starting games of tag and kickball, even if I sucked at them. I weaseled my way into the clusters of friend groups that scattered the schoolyard. But no matter how fully I entrenched myself into the inner circle, I was always left orbiting it, like an asteroid broken from the pack. Space junk, third wheeling and catching up.

What was the cause? I asked myself. *Was it my clothes? Was I not smart enough? Or too smart? Was I too pushy...? Or not pushy enough?*

I addressed these questions, like a scientist trying to prove a theory, one by one. In controlled experiments, I made myself malleable, to fit into the mold of any situation necessary. If they wanted smart, they got her. If they wanted chill, they got her. If they wanted assertive, they got her. But after trial and failure, it never worked.

So... maybe... it was something else. Something I wanted to keep buried, locked up, the key thrown away. But at every turn, someone was jerking that key back into the hole, nagging at my one weakness.

Was it my hair? Tied up into a tight puff at the top of my head, something my mother took pride in, but I hated.

"What do you guys wanna do for recess today?" I asked my two friends, Rosalind and Hope. "We play that ninja game *every day*, I'm getting kinda tired of it."

As I spoke, Rosalind put a hand over her mouth, held in a laugh. I looked at Hope in confusion, then back at her. "What? What is it? Is there something on my face?"

My head jerked back, almost throwing me off balance and onto the floor. A few seconds later, my scalp burned where my hair had been yanked. When I regained my footing, I pivoted to see Nishit, my ex-best friend, and his minions laughing at me. "Leave me alone, freak, or I'll get Mrs. Handler," I spat.

They took off for the playground, chortling like villains in a movie.

I remembered the conflict between our little friend groups got so bad that in the fifth grade my teacher had to gather us all together in an intervention to get them to stop. And, somehow, the jokes directed at me were always about my appearance, my hair or even my skin. Nope, it couldn't be that.

Maybe it was that one time, the first day of school in music class, where my teacher had us do icebreakers. One of the questions was whether you lived in an apartment, or in a house. And when I said 'House,' the kids cocked their heads, surprised. Nah, must be something else.

It was probably my clothes, always attempting to model the popular girls but never quite making it. I mentioned that my shoes were from Payless one day, and the class erupted in laughter. Never wore them again. But that shouldn't be it, no.

The way I spoke *couldn't* be the answer because I spoke just like the other kids. Even made an effort to pay attention to grammar, and to correct those that used it improperly. I remember a girl telling me that she was 'blacker than me' for using 'ain't' when she spoke. But that was a *good* thing, that I spoke well. That I didn't use incorrect words like 'ain't,' words that weren't in the real dictionary, made-up words. They couldn't *possibly* dislike me for that.

Or was it my skin? The skin that everyone swiveled in their chairs to look at when we learned about slavery in history class? That was always compared to chocolate and cinnamon, but also, dog shit and dirt. No, it *couldn't* be that. Because schools taught inclusivity of all races, and it's not like anyone had said anything explicitly *racist*. It's not like they'd walked right up to me and said, "We don't like you because you're black." Right? *Right*.

Being Muslim, going to the mosque and Sunday School every weekend, I found a group of people with a few shared traits. A core pillar of Islam is acceptance of all races, backgrounds, and ethnicities into the religion. But even then, the kids at Sunday school were Pakistani and Indian. They spoke in languages I couldn't understand and ate food that I'd never tried. Inside and outside of the classroom, I was the black sheep.

My parents made humble attempts to connect me to our culture. We'd attend festivals and concerts in Chicago annually, getting a glimpse of the lives of people that looked like us. But at the end of the day, we would get back into our minivan and return to our little suburb, far from the city and its diversity. Always apart, detached from the whole.

I was stuck in limbo. Always balancing on the edge of having friends, and not. School wasn't always miserable, though. There were definitely good times, times where I could let go of some of the personas I'd masked myself in. The faces I would put on to pretend I didn't care about the bullying, or the loneliness, or the otherization. But they never *all* fell at once. Because if they did, what would be left underneath?

"Your bra straps are showing," she said abruptly, still looking down at the computer screen.

I scrambled to tuck them away, as she tilted the webcam on her computer towards my face. Before I could stand up straight, a photo snapped, and an ID card was printed out seconds later.

She handed it to me with a grunt, along with my schedule on a piece of paper.

I analyzed it, as I left the small front office. I hated that photo. You could see where my bra straps were tucked into my shirt, rolled up over my collarbones. A hollow smile plastered on my face, weighing down my cheeks. It was a fake smile, of course, because that's what you do when someone shoves a camera in your face. Or when you just don't wanna be in a new city, at a new school, right in the middle of the year.

I wandered around campus for a few minutes. I was already late for first period, Honors English, in more ways than one. We'd moved well into the first semester, so my peers already knew each other and had adjusted to their classes. What was the point in trying to make friends—everyone was already well-situated with their cliques and friend groups. I'd only make myself a burden, a third wheel.

Before entering the room, I scanned my carefully curated outfit: Ripped jeans, a floral tank top, feathered earrings. My hair was in a braid-out, perfect coils that took hours of combing and weaving and moisturizing. I had my new shoes, too, a pair of olive-green Vans, something I never wore in Chicago but noticed were a trend here, in California, so I splurged. I even had on lip gloss, something I only pulled out for the *big* occasions. I probably wouldn't make friends, but I might as well try to make a good first impression.

I knocked precariously on the ajar door. Immediately, all these new faces looked up at me... but... they were shrouded in witches' hats... and clown wigs... *What?* Even the teacher, in a... *blue princess dress?*

Oh.

I'm so stupid.

It was Halloween.

The old keyboards had tall buttons, producing loud, ugly clacking noises that distracted my train of thought. The aroma of a dozen lunches wafted into my nostrils in a weird funk, just annoying. Why should eating be allowed in a library? They could get food on the books.

All of the chair legs bent outwards, tangling with the network of wires underneath the ancient computers. I always had to fight my way to get a seat, before the seventh-grade boys ran in to play their video games. Sometimes, I'd get a seat in the corner, squeezed on both sides. There was nowhere to put my backpack—I couldn't leave it on the ground to be tripped over. So, I sat with it, on the edge of my chair, hunched over the computer for half an hour.

I hated my new city, and its new smells and its new people and its new ways of doing things. Things that everyone felt normal doing but felt foreign to me. Even some of the words that they used were different, accents a bit tweaked. So, I went to the library at lunch, sat alone in the corner, and wrote my book. I couldn't make friends in the real world, but my characters could do whatever I wanted them to. I could transport myself into another world, a simulation where I have all the control, blocking out all my surroundings. Sounds muffled around me, tunnel vision. It was just me and the page, me, and my characters...

Until the bell rang.

I rose from my haze. Lunch was over, everyone around me jerked up from their seats and took off. Passing period was only a few minutes, and the school was big. If you lingered too long, you'd end up late. And my next class was on the other side of the school. I dragged the mouse to the X in the top right corner and logged out. Until tomorrow.

I wrote a lot in my first months of moving to Silicon Valley, holding on to the one thing I loved while everything else was thousands of miles away. My writing morphed, though. I found myself gravitating towards subjects of fantasy and fiction, things that couldn't possibly exist in the real world. But I was often burnt out, feeling passionate about my story and then just... *not*.

That first day... Halloween, with all my peers in costumes. That wasn't the only reason I stood out from them. Even still being a minority myself, the region of California that I was now in was quite diverse. For the first time in my life, white people were not in the majority. And that was very unbelievable to me.

Growing up around white people, reading books with white characters, watching movies with white actors... I look now and think, *Why in* Hell *would I write a black character?* It only took leaving a white-dominated city to see it. To see that I had zero connection to black culture: black culture as foreign to me as writing an Asian character, or a queer or trans* character. Writing black characters felt like an invasion of a community I simply didn't belong to. So, in the year that we moved, my eighth grade, I wrote an urban fantasy novel with a white girl called Alexandra Leandros as the lead, because that was the demographic I thought I needed to write in.

There were a multitude of reasons as to why my writing sucked: static characters, undeveloped worldbuilding, unexplainable plot holes. But the biggest reason I felt disconnected from my writing was because I wasn't writing a *real* character. I was writing the shell of a character that I *wanted* to exist, just like my personality that I *wanted* to project to the world. I was writing a character with the personas I'd applied to myself over the years. And we all know how good I was at that.

I loved everything about my story, all the flaws I couldn't see then, but were glaringly obvious now. Everything *except* the main character. Believe me, I *wanted* to like her. It made sense to want to like her; she was a projection of all the things I wanted to be: effortlessly confident, carefree, a magnet to social interaction. I'm a try hard, I put in too much effort. She was a free spirit, letting the friends come to her. I'm a stoic, blunt and harsh. She was an optimist, bubbly and endearing.

No matter how much I tried to differentiate her from me, we were essentially the same. Both fragments of a whole, onions without rings. And I *hated* how transparently obvious that was. At the end of middle school, I scrapped that story, and took a hiatus from writing that lasted longer than intended. Because instead of being able to channel my jumbled emotions and thoughts into a plot, into characters that were just idealized versions of myself—I knew I had to *face them*. My one true passion was being stained by my internal issues, and that, I couldn't let happen. Writing wasn't like my other masks, recyclable, and disposable.

Writing was what *was* underneath it all, the only thing left when it all came crashing down. I couldn't discard it. I had to fix it.

I was so sick and tired of the personas, the facades. Having moved was physically, mentally, and emotionally exhaustive, and I didn't need the struggle of social interaction weighing me down. So instead of making friends, I developed tunnel vision: grades, assignments, academic success, rinse and repeat. I saw no need for meaningless social interaction when there were essays to write, tests to ace, exams to study for.

It was hard, trying to strike a balance. Because no matter how much I despised the attempt to make friends, I knew I *needed* them. I was jealous of the kids in their groups at lunch, of the inside jokes and the boisterous laughs.

Moving *was* exhausting—but that exhaust was just what I needed. I was too tired to carry my masks, so I let them fall. A new school, a new group of people—all with no prior knowledge of me and my mistakes. I could've tried any mask I wanted, and it probably would've worked. But I chose *no mask*, to be my raw, unfiltered self. I did what I wanted with no regard for others' opinions of it, liberation from self-constructed restraints that tied me down for too long.

It still didn't work.

By the end of sophomore year, after putting myself out there for the first time, being my true self... I had no friends to show for it all.

Of course, a couple people stuck here and there. But no one with *those inside jokes*, with *those boisterous laughs*. I had acquaintances, people I could chat about the surface-level stuff with. This is where things started to take a turn for the worse. Because my calculated efforts at trial and failure that I'd been putting into practice for nearly half a decade *simply weren't working*. All I've ever been told from teachers and mentors and parents is that "You can make friends, if you try hard enough! Just join some clubs, put yourself out there!" I *did* put myself out there. I *did* join the clubs. I'd *tried*, believe me. I've tried in every single color and shape and form imaginable. Nothing.

For a long time after that, I blamed myself. I mean, Einstein said it best—The definition of insanity is doing the same thing over and over again and expecting different results. It was clearly *my* fault. I was conducting the experiment wrong.

Or... were my variables skewed?

You can ask anyone, despite age or race or gender, "What was the weirdest year of your life?" and 2020 will top their list. 2020 was no different for me, setting me on a trajectory that I would've never walked.

It was June 7th, a mellow Sunday afternoon, when I opened Instagram for the fifth time that day, scrolling aimlessly for something to distract me from my serious writer's block. Anaya—an acquaintance of mine—had a new post on her story: A Black Lives Matter protest, at three o'clock, at the local police department. With nothing better to do, I grabbed my phone and went.

We marched around the city with a succession of police cars and news outlets on our tail, people with big cameras and microphones to document the event. Anaya got up on a makeshift podium, standing in the bed of a pickup truck. She narrated a poem about her sorrow for the death of George Floyd, and other black people in my community got up after her, talking about their experiences with racism. I didn't know how similar we all were. I didn't know how we all got *those* thoughts in the back of our heads, that *Maybe I'm disliked because I'm black. Maybe I'm looked at differently because I'm black. Maybe I'm all alone because I'm black.*

Being young, seeing the deaths of black people on the TV, or in articles, it felt a bit desensitizing at times. Sometimes, there was a new story every other week about a black person getting shot on the street. And I really asked myself *What does this have to do with me?*

The racism that I face is very different from George Floyd's and Breonna Taylor's, making it difficult to identify with them that summer. My racism is like a single thread woven into a sheet with ten-thousand count. It was *passive-aggressive*, all judgmental looks, assumptions, and stereotypes. And yes, it was *no friends*.

There were people at the protest talking about the big issues—police brutality, mass incarceration, discrimination—the reasons we were all there. But there were also people talking about things that hit closer to home—being followed by security guards for no reason, being ostracized at school, seeing people talk about you behind your back. Things that I, as the average black person, have actually felt and could connect to. Knowing that some of the inconsistencies in the way that I'm treated aren't because of me as a *person*, but me as a *black person*, somehow made things easier. It removed the burden on myself, and my personas, to make up for a flaw that was out of my control. Honestly, it was relieving.

I lost hope in my ability to ever be a part of that "inner circle," to be accepted by others, whether I discarded my masks or not. I conceded to the fact that friendship might not come to me, so maybe I shouldn't try to seek it. Not entirely, but selectively, in places where no amount of effort or patience or cultivation would bring me the results I wanted. I learned instead that it was useless of me to seek any sort of validation from people that *aren't of my same skin color*. Because no attention I seek to gain will *ever* erase me of my exterior. My *black* exterior. No variety of personas, extracurriculars, skills, and personalities will ever make up for the fact that *I am a black person*, at least not in the eyes of those who aren't. The only people who will ever understand that are other black people. So maybe I should focus my efforts on them.

The red paint has a thicker consistency than the white and blue, so I slap it on in wide stripes, pressing the brush down, deep into the canvas. Then the navy blue, the orange, the brown, and finally the black. Half an hour later it was done—my quickest painting yet.

Something about the rage in me must've made my hands go faster.

It was a painting of the American flag, something I'd never had the desire to draw until now. Even then, it wasn't in its normal, patriotic form—I'd interlaced the stripes of red with flames, tangling orange in those red lines like vines. No longer star-spangled, I'd replaced the fifty states with one phrase in black ink: Black Lives Matter. And finally, in the foreground, the side profile of a black person, brown skin and curly hair, the phrase serving as a text bubble for their words.

I thought about being back in Chicago, when that girl had told me she was "blacker than me" for speaking in African American Vernacular English, the slang that I'd looked down upon. I didn't feel validated then. I didn't feel elevated in my status as a black person, being better at grammar than even a white girl. I didn't feel the way I *thought* I'd feel: White myself.

Whether I knew it or not, I've been spending the past decade trying to yank and twist and bend myself to fit every mold imaginable—and those molds were white. Those personas, those masks—they were all of white people. People that I wanted to be but never could. The characters that I'd crafted in my stories, in my fictional world that I believed to be totally free of outside control—*they were all white.*

White is a clean color, it's the symbol of purity. But my entire identity has been tainted by its control. My entire life has been directed toward a path of attaining that color, reaching that bright beacon in the sky that's just out of reach. I've just now learned that I'll *never* get there. And now it's about being okay with that.

I've started writing again, after a long time. My current work is a dystopian science fiction, with Marcel as my main character, a black boy with educated parents. They push him to pursue a life like theirs: to reach out to that white beacon in the sky, to make it his success story. Marcel listens to his parents, he puts on that mask, just as I did. But did he make the right choice?

I guess you'll have to read to find out.

In My Court
by Erikah Sanders, Age 13

Chapter 1 - Nevaeh

Thursday

The class bell rings, signaling that I should go to Chemistry class. I groan and tell my tennis teammates at the Quad goodbye and head to my next class. I hope this class is quick so I can get to the tennis court to practice my backhand swing.

I see my friend Claire also walking to my class, so I join her. During Chemistry, we are given a new group assignment to start the annual science fair project. Of course, getting your groups assigned by the teacher is one of the worst situations a student could ever have. Thankfully, she pairs me with Claire but also with another girl that I am suspicious about. Her name is Simone. I have heard things about Simone that make me stay alert. Claire is in almost all of my classes, so I know her very well and we are good friends. But I don't know Simone at all. Once Ms. Stark reads off all the group names, everyone splits up and gets to work. Simone and Claire come up to my desk for us to all work together.

I greet Simone. "Nice to meet you! My name is Nevaeh."

But she snaps back with, "I didn't ask what your name was. We are here to work on this project and win. And if we are going to win, then I should be the leader, and everyone needs to listen to me."

"I think Nevaeh should be the leader," says Claire, "because she has the best Chemistry grade, and she knows what she is talking about…"

Simone rolls her eyes at the both of us and looks away.

Thankfully, the class bell rings, and I start to leave the class without hesitation. I grab my bag and my tennis racket, but Simone sees me alone in the hallway.

"You're nothing compared to me. Even though Claire wanted you to be the group leader, it doesn't matter because she doesn't know anything either! You both are under my rules whether you like it or not."

"What did I ever do to you?" I respond. "I don't even know you like that! And leave me alone before I get you in trouble."

"I don't care if you try to get me in trouble because I *never* get in trouble," she snaps back. "This is why black people shouldn't be in school. They're unteachable, overdramatic, lazy and get terrible grades."

My mind explodes, but I stay calm and think there are two different paths from here. I can either walk away from the situation or I can act 'ghetto' in the hallway. After a deep breath, I walk away because if I were to act 'ghetto' then I would have proven her point. That black people are overdramatic.

I grab my bags and my tennis racket and head to the curb where my dad picks me up to take me to tennis practice. I get in the car without a word, and he thankfully gives me space through the entire ride.

I run to my friends on the court and we bump rackets as a 'hello.' We trash talk each other about how one of us is gonna win and is better than all of us. That's the way that we show affection for each other. As soon as Coach calls us over to start warm-ups and then play a match, I feel the stress from school lift off my shoulders.

2 Hours Later...

"Nevaeh, are you ready yet?" Dad yells.

I'm packing my bags from practice. "Ugh, give me a moment. Let me just pack up all my stuff." I hate how it gets hot and I start sweating. It makes me feel so disgusting, but I love the way that I can be so competitive and not hurt anyone's feelings because... it's just a game. When my tennis racket drags on the ground, I notice a new scrape. Like who has the time to pick up a racket, hold it, and actually carry it to the car. Not only putting it in the car and making sure it doesn't fall off the seat but bringing it in the house. So, I just drag it.

Dad interrupts my thoughts. "Nevaeh come on! I don't have all day! And neither do you because of your heavy load of homework tonight!"

As this tennis racket gets heavier, so do my thoughts about what happened at school today.

Getting in the car is just like the tennis court; I hate it, but I love it so much. When Dad turns up his 80s and 90s jams, it embarrasses me even though it's just us in the car. But on the other hand, sometimes I get to play my current R&B and Hip Hop. He pretends to love it but inside I can tell he hates it. Parents are weird that way.

When we finally get home after music jams and traffic jams, the first thing he does is take off his shoes, place them by the door, and head straight to the kitchen to make me a Thursday Deluxe PB&J.

"How was your day, love bug?" he asks.

"It was all right," I say. But when I speak in that tone, it *obviously* isn't all right.

"Are you sure? You can talk to me about anything."

"Dad! I said I'm fine. And if it was something, I can handle it on my own anyway."

"Okay, whatever you say. Just know that I'm here for you." Dad has a special skill. He always knows when someone is not truly expressing how they are feeling inside.

I end the conversation by going up to my room to think about what happened at school. I don't want to talk about it with anyone except my sister Camella because I know if I tell anyone else, they would make a big deal out of it. But not Camella, she would comfort me and figure out how we should deal with it together.

As I dial her phone, I anxiously wait for her to pick up. "Come on! Pick up, pick up, pick up already!" I whisper to myself.

She finally answers. "Hello? What's up little sis!"

"Ah nothing much. What are you doing today?" I pray she doesn't say that she's busy.

"Oh nothing. I'm going to hang around the house. I had a long week so I decided to take the day off."

My prayers have been answered. "Great! Is it okay if I have Dad drop me off at your place? I really need to talk to you about something and if I talk about it with Dad, well, you know how he gets." I'm already thinking in my head how Dad is going to grill me about why I want to be dropped off at my sister's house.

"Wait Nevaeh, actually, Dad might be an obstacle to get past so just tell him that I will pick you up instead."

"Okay cool. Thanks again!" I hang up the phone and I finally start to feel a sense of relief that everything is going to be okay, and I have nothing to worry about. Well, for now.

I tell Dad that Camella will be here soon to pick me up.

"Okay honey, have fun and be safe!" He actually had one of the most surprising reactions I've ever heard! Now, I kind of regret not telling him but like I said, Camella won't start anything, but she will definitely help me end it.

Loud music blasts outside and I already know it's my sister. She gets that from Dad. She stands out of the sunroof waving and screaming. It looks kinda funny when she does that and that's why the neighbors don't really appreciate it when she comes around.

"Aye Nevaeh, get in!" she yells.

"Okay, coming now!" I scream back.

When I walk into her new apartment, her new dog Lola sprints to the door and starts barking at me. The stance in her short, long

Chihuahua body tells me that she doesn't like me. I knew that Camella had a dog, but not a bodyguard. I bend down to pet her and she immediately comes to sniff and lick my hand. After that we are friends.

"Can we talk about the thing?" I ask.

"Yes. Let's sit at the kitchen table," Camella responds.

We both sit at the table.

"So, what happened?"

I take a deep breath and share the argument I had with Simone.

"Oh my goodness!" Camella says. "This is not okay! Does she not know what is going on in the world today with all of the racial injustice? Has she not learned anything? Take me to her and she will for sure leave you alone after meeting me!"

"See, this is what I didn't want. I wanted you to give me advice, not step in."

"Okay whatever, but I'm here if you want me to handle it. But if not, what I would do is tell Ms. Johnson. Two years ago, I had a similar interaction at the high school, and she was always someone that I felt good talking to if I needed support. Tell her that I'm your sister too just so she knows who you are."

"I will try to find her tomorrow. Thank you so much!"

"No problem! And I'm really sorry that this happened. If you need to talk again, I'm just a call away." She gives me a hug.

I've always loved her hugs even though I act like I don't. Just like tennis.

Friday

All through the first period, my mind is racing about what Ms. Johnson would be like. Whenever I talk about my teachers around Camella, she always says, "Oh my God, I remember them! They were so nice and kind to me." But how come when I talk to my teachers just to be friendly, I get a lecture and extra homework? Maybe Camella has that *special* touch.

I head straight to the teacher's lounge after class, hoping to see Ms. Johnson (kids aren't usually allowed in there so if she's not there, I'm gonna look really stupid). When I open the door, I see a dark, African American, heavy-set woman standing by the coffee maker, laughing with the history teacher, Mr. Alvarado.

"Excuse me? Are you Ms. Johnson?" I ask.

"Yes, I am!" Ms. Johnson says. "Now what can I do for you? Oh wait! Are you Camella's little sister?"

I hesitate. "Yup, I am. My name is Nevaeh. And Camella told me to come see you because I had a racial conflict yesterday. She said that maybe you could help."

Ms. Johnson suggests, "Do you want to go to my classroom and talk about it?"

"Yes, that would be great," I say.

We walk over to her classroom, sit down at her desk and I repeat what happened. I start tearing up, it feels like I'm reliving it all over again.

"Aw, don't cry." She hands me the tissue box. "Everything is going to be okay so don't worry about any of this. This is not my first time dealing with this. Thank you for coming to me."

I feel so safe hearing that from Ms. Johnson. I feel that she understands what I am going through, even more than my mom would. Mom is never home anymore. It's always just my dad and me. When she is home, she comes in, grabs more money and some food, and then leaves again. She claims that she's at work all the time but since she doesn't make that much money, like from a big-time job, I think something is up. But I leave it alone and pretend nothing is wrong.

Ms. Johnson hugs me and tells me, "Everything will be okay. I know some other African American kids that have come to me about Simone. She has insulted people because of the color of their skin and has started fights. You, me and Simone will definitely have a private conversation about this incident because this is unacceptable."

Chapter 2 – Simone

Friday

Every day I make an excuse to stay with the English teacher, Ms. Giordani. She is the only teacher I feel comfortable hanging out with because she feels like the mother I never had. Or the *parents* that I never had.

"How was your day, Simone?" Ms. Giordani asks.

"It was okay, not the best day at school," I reply.

"Oh no! Do you want to talk about what happened?"

"Nope. I'm okay. I have to go, Ms. G, see you tomorrow."

"Okay. Text me when you get home and see you tomorrow!"

I'm walking home... all by myself. Under the sparkly night sky. I get home safely so I text Ms. G. It would be so much easier if one of my parents just picked me up from school once in a while. I live with my mom. Mom and Dad have been divorced since the middle of my sixth-grade year. I really don't know who to go to if I need anything.

Instead of stressing myself out about how my parents are non-existent, I think about what happened at school today. I say to myself, *"Why did I do that?! I said so many rude and disrespectful things to her! I feel bad about all the other people too and I didn't even mean what I said! It was all out of anger!"* If my mom finds out, she would be furious with me and wouldn't support what I did. She would say, "You did it, so you have to deal with it." But if my dad finds out, I will have to switch schools and then I wouldn't get to spend time with Ms. G. And if I leave, I can't sincerely apologize to all the people I've hurt along the way. Dad already knows that I am constantly being rude to other people because of my anger and frustration.

Today at school, it wasn't even just Nevaeh who made me so mad but Claire's suggestions. Nevaeh already has a lot of friends, amazing parents that support her, a sister that cares for her, so why does she need to be the leader too? I have no friends (except Ms. G), parents who don't notice me, and siblings who don't want to talk to me or hang out with me when they have the time. All I want is to be heard and to be the leader. But I guess I can't have that either. I feel like my head is about to explode! I would scream but I guess no one would care.

Saturday

It's the weekend and I feel that it's not gonna be very fun. Usually on the weekends I play on my Wii U and computer all day and only get up to get food and go to the bathroom. But this time, I keep getting up because I am *actually* tired of playing Mario Kart and Super Smash Bros. That's how I know that something is wrong with me. I can't stop thinking about what I did to Nevaeh. I want to call her and apologize, but I don't have her number. It's better to apologize in person anyway; to show that I really mean it.

Sunday

"Simone, go put away these dishes right now!" Mom says. "Then cook dinner and after that you can clean the kitchen too! You weren't put in this world to just sit around and play video games all day. You have to share the household duties. Also, why aren't you doing your homework?"

"Yes Mom, I know. I know that I need to put away the dishes, cook, clean, and do homework." I roll my eyes and sarcastically ask, "Is there anything else you want me to do?"

"Well, not for the next two hours!" she replies. "Go ahead and do your chores!"

I head up to my room after my chores, still thinking about Nevaeh. Does she have to do all these unnecessary chores on the weekend too? Oh, wait; I forget. She has the perfect parents, the perfect sibling, and the perfect life. I'm positive she doesn't have to do all these chores.

Chapter 3 – Nevaeh

Monday

I feel ready to talk to Simone about what she did. I see Ms. Johnson and she signals me over.

"Are you ready to talk to Simone?"

"Yup! I feel more ready than ever!"

"Okay, let me bring Simone to my classroom so we can have a discussion," Ms. Johnson says.

As I'm replaying in my mind what Simone said to me, Ms. Johnson walks through the door with her hand resting on Simone's shoulder. I turn my head and Simone gives me a mean mug. I thought that she would come in crying and instantly regretting what she did. But nope. She's still fearless.

"Simone, Nevaeh came and told me what you said to her," Ms. Johnson says. "Would you like to explain what you were thinking and why you did it?"

I can't believe what comes next.

Simone slowly breaks down into tears. "I am so sorry, Nevaeh. I didn't mean for any of this to happen. I was so stressed and jealous of you that I felt like I had to say something mean just to express my feelings. You have a lot of friends, amazing parents and mine hardly notice me."

I think to myself, *I want to trust her, but the fact that she has hurt multiple people multiple times, doesn't make this situation feel any different. The kindness in me says, "It was just an accident. She didn't mean it and it came out of her anger. Give her another chance and forgive her." But the mistrust in me says, "If it was an accident, why would she not say sorry right after she said it. Also, she mean-mugged me after she came into the room. Since she wasn't apologetic at all, you shouldn't forgive her."*

But I remember vividly from three tennis classes ago what my teacher told me: "Tennis is just a game. Just like life. But all you need to do to win, is to trust your gut and be proud of the decisions you make. Whether it's choosing a backhand over a forehand or making a decision that will change your life forever, I trust that you will play your cards correctly." So, I choose kindness.

"I understand where you are coming from. It is still hard for me to believe you, but I guess I'll give you another chance. I'm sorry you went through that type of stuff. Also, I wanted to work it out just between the two of us, but I didn't know if you would insult me again, so I felt like I needed to tell someone to help us deal with the situation."

"Yes, I totally agree. Do you think we can start over again? And maybe even become friends?" Simone asks.

I take a deep breath and say, "Yes! Hello! My name is Nevaeh! What is your name?"

"Hello! I'm Simone."

We shake hands and go to our next class.

Tuesday

Simone waits by the courtyard for me. We walk to class together

"Hey, do you want a ride home from school today?" I ask.

She starts to cry. "Yes, thank you so much."

Thursday

I take a deep breath and I ask Simone for the fourth time if she can do her part for the science fair.

"Oh, I will do it later."

I bet "later" ends up being a whole week! I let her be the leader of the group for a day or two but all she did was abuse her power by sitting around and telling us what to do!

The bell rings and we walk to the parking lot. I see my dad and I tell her, "Try not to eat in his car. He gets really mad when there are crumbs everywhere in his new car. He had to vacuum the seats last time and he was already mad at me. So, let's not have him be mad again!"

"It's all right!" Simone says. "I won't get any crumbs anywhere. Trust me, I'm not as messy as my brothers."

We both laugh it off and get in the car.

As soon as she pulls out her lunch box, my dad turns around and looks at me like, 'Umm you better tell her to stop before I do.'

After I tell her to stop, she says, "Oh it's fine, I won't make a mess." But by the time she gets out of the car it smells like old enchiladas and there are goldfish crumbs everywhere!

"Dad, I am so sorry for her behavior. She is just getting used to having friends, so she doesn't know how to act. She doesn't listen to me. I really don't want to be her friend anymore, but I don't want to hurt her feelings."

"Nevaeh, why did you even become friends with her?" Dad questions. "I know you don't like tennis references, but it seems like she is volleying with your emotions! At first you enjoyed her company and now you wish that you weren't friends to begin with."

"That's the part I didn't tell you. Do you remember that time I called Camella over to pick me up? That was the day when Simone said some very racist things to me. A teacher that was a friend of Camella's helped straighten the problem out. But I wanted to give her a second chance because I felt bad for her and the environment that she lives in."

"You need to stay true to yourself," Dad responds. "Ask yourself, 'Do I feel the need to be friends with her, or do I want to?' It's hard dealing with someone who doesn't understand you, so you have to do what is best for you, Nevaeh."

Chapter 4 – Simone

Monday

Now that I'm friends with Nevaeh, I feel that I have turned over a new leaf. With a friend like Nevaeh liking and supporting me for who I am, life is starting to get better. I am much happier, and I don't mistreat people anymore. And I am definitely not disrespecting other kids because of their race. I know that was so wrong of me. I really don't know what life would be like without her and I'm glad it's not like that anymore. Ever since the word spread that Nevaeh and I are friends it feels like more people are ready to give me a chance. Even some of the popular kids are starting to talk to me. If it wasn't for Nevaeh, I most likely would have switched schools and had to start over again. My future looks so much brighter. I really do hope that Nevaeh feels the same way about me.

I walk to room A32 for Chemistry and Nevaeh is in there talking to Claire and some boy I don't recognize. "Hey Nevaeh and Claire!" I say, as I walk in. "Are you guys ready to ace this science fair project? Also, who's this guy?"

"Oh him?" Nevaeh responds. "This is Sam. He's one of my best friends from kindergarten. He goes to St. Jose High School."

"Hello, Sam, nice to meet you!"

"Hello Simone, nice to meet you too!"

I leave the classroom and sit right outside the door in the hallway to get some quiet work time. I hear the bell, so I go inside the classroom to sit in my seat. After we finish our presentation, I go back to my seat wondering what my grade is gonna be.

Chapter 5 – Nevaeh

Monday

Today is the day that we present our science fair project to the class. I think Claire and I will do well, but butterflies grow in my stomach from the fear of Simone not presenting well.

Ms. Stark calls us up and Claire and I present professionally, showing great confidence, while Simone reads her part like she didn't get any sleep for the past two weeks. Ugh! Since we all are being graded the same, I bet Simone ruined our perfect score.

Ms. Stark hands out grades to everyone in my group and I can see from the corner of my eye that Simone did not get the same grade as Claire and me. I can see that her rubric grade says C-.

Simone looks ashamed so she goes up to Ms. Stark with her paper in her hand. "Hello Ms. Stark, why did my group and I get such a low grade?" she asks. "I thought that we did pretty good."

"It was actually just your grade," Ms. Stark responds. "I know you could have put more effort into it. It seemed like you didn't care about the grade and that your teammates didn't matter. It didn't seem like you were part of a team. I hope this is a lesson that you should be more prepared for presentations in the future."

Simone walks back to her seat, shoves her paper into her backpack and walks out the door without saying goodbye to anyone. After seeing her rude reaction, I remember what I promised myself after talking to my dad, which is to stay true to myself and do what is best for me. I see Simone in the hallway and I approach her. "We need to talk now," I say. "It's urgent and I hope it doesn't shake you up, but it's important."

Simone gets up and follows me to the courtyard.

"All right, being your friend has been really hard on me lately," I say. "I know you try to be a great friend, but you never listen to me. For example, I told you to not eat in my dad's car and you still did anyways. He got very mad at me and it wasn't even my fault because I *told* you in the first place not to eat in his car. You also abused your power when we agreed that you could be the leader for the science fair presentation by just yelling at Claire and me to tell us what to do."

She nods her head like she understands, but I don't think she does.

"I don't think this friendship is gonna work," I tell her. "I'm so sorry but I can't be in a friendship where I am not happy." I get up and walk away feeling proud that I finally got it off my chest, but feel like a jerk because I know I broke Simone's heart.

Simone gets up and leaves.

I go to the curb where everyone gets picked up and I see Sam. I run up to him and hug him because I want to be reminded of what a great friendship feels like. I think he can tell that I'm hurting, so he makes me laugh.

I text my dad and he pulls his car up right in front of Simone. I push my way through the crowd to get into my dad's car. He rolls down the window to talk to Simone, but I quickly say, "Dad, just drive."

Killer Kids
by Jolie Wilson, Age 15

After a long drive with my parents' personal driver, I finally arrived at the front of my school. Man, I hated that place. It's full of snobby and stuck-up rich kids who don't know how to keep their secrets and opinions to themselves.

I shook my hair one last time, making sure my loose curls sat naturally and not flattened from leaning back during the car ride.

"Hey, princess!" some random student greeted me.

"My name is Saige," I mumbled. I should be used to it since it seemed to be my nickname around here.

After I walked into my classroom, I was surprised to be greeted by a substitute teacher. Everyone flooded in after me and they seemed to be just as surprised as I was. I took my seat in the back of the class right beside the window.

"What's up, princess?" Julian, my seatmate greeted me.

"That's not my name. Why does everyone call me that?" I asked.

"Well, you're pretty much the wealthiest person in this school. It only fits." The boy shrugged, before he leant back in his seat and put his feet on the desk in front of him.

"No. It does not fit. Princesses are weak and helpless people who depend on other people to solve their own problems. I for one am not that type of person," I stated. Before Julian could say another word, I faced forward and quickly put in my ear buds...

And Julian ripped them back out.

"I'm sorry to ask, but do you mind giving me the answers to last night's homework? I had football practice," he said.

Without answering I quickly took out last night's homework and slid it to Julian before going back to what I was busy doing before.

"Hello everyone! My name is Mrs. Brown and I'll be your teacher while Mrs. Davis is on maternity leave." The substitute teacher's voice boomed throughout the room and caused all heads to turn towards her. Her head, though, suddenly turned towards Julian. Mrs. Davis probably had told her about Julian's reputation for being disruptive. "I am very strict and observant about how things are done, and I won't let things go easily like your last teacher did," she continued. She then pointed to a list of rules that were written on the board, but everyone seemed to ignore them. "Now class, pass your homework to the front, and turn to page 43 in your textbooks."

About twenty minutes into class, there I was listening to music while I pretended to read the assigned pages. That was until Mrs. Brown quickly snatched my earphones.

"What is your name, dear?" she asked.

"Saige Kim."

"Detention, you obviously didn't read the rules that I have here on the board."

"Who did?" Julian asked, sarcastically.

"And you can go right along with her. As I see you are copying notes, which is not allowed," she snapped back.

Julian glared at the teacher with his hazel eyes while poking his tongue in his cheeks. His curly light brown hair covered them slightly.

I turned my head away and realized that I'd been staring for too long.

"You two meet me in room 108. After school," she added before she walked to the front of the room again.

I sat at a half empty table in the middle of the cafeteria. I put in my extra pair of earphones and observed everyone like I usually did. No, it's not creepy because what else can you do when you have no friends? It's not like I wanted friends anyway.

Arguing came from the table next to me and I couldn't help but pry. Trey Jones was arguing with Jazmine Kennedy. The argument escalated quickly when water was poured all over the boy. "Oohs" and "Aahs" were heard all over the cafeteria and gained not only the attention of the students, but of the teachers too.

"Jazmine Kennedy! Detention after school!" A teacher shouted. Jazmine sighed out in frustration and practically stomped her way out the cafeteria, pushing everyone in her way.

One of the teachers cooed before guiding him out of the cafetaria. "Trey, let's go ahead and get you a dry uniform, you poor baby."

Everyone started snickering at Trey and his physical state. He was not the most likeable out there since he was such a teacher's pet. He was drenched in water and his glasses were all foggy. His thick and curly hair absorbed most of the water though.

I walked into room 108 where I and all the other detainees were supposed to serve our sentence. I was the first to arrive, so I chose a random seat and pulled out all my homework to complete in the two hours given.

Jazmine walked in soon after me, too engrossed in her phone to realize that someone else was present in the room.

The clicking of her acrylic nails onto her phone distracted me from my work. "Um, Jazmine. Do you mind?"

Her blue eyes looked up from her phone and directly into my hazel ones. She gave a short glare before continuing typing away. I shouldn't have been surprised.

Not too long after, Julian walked in and sat right beside me, despite the many available seats in the room. "Hey, princess."

I ignored him of course.

Mrs. Brown walked in along with Jacob, and this other kid who I'd never seen before. He took a seat in the front of the class near the door.

"These two will be monitoring you guys while I finish some paperwork. You guys' task is to clean off the chalkboard, all the desks, chairs and floors and don't forget the gum all over the ceiling. If I see one piece of gum left, you'll all be called back for another detention," Mrs. Brown warned before she pulled out a clipboard on which I assumed our names were.

Trey soon lay down the rules. The only one who seemed to be paying attention was the boy.

"Hey," I greeted the boy. Everyone's attention was on him now. "What's your name?" I asked politely.

"Ben Russo," he said quietly, but still loud enough for everyone to hear in the silent room.

I recognized the last name. My parents once worked with his dad but soon cut things off. They'd claimed that the man was crazy and money hungry.

"Saige Kim," I greeted and stuck out my hand for him to shake.

To my surprise he glared at me and decided to ignore my friendly gesture.

"It's because of my parents and your dad, isn't it? The reason you're now ignoring me after I told you my name?"

All he did was shrug and face forward.

"Oooh, tough. The one time you try to be nice the person ends up ignoring you. How does it feel, princess?" Julian snickered.

"Enough talking," Trey called out.

After we all grabbed our own supplies, we gave each other separate duties for cleaning. We put Ben in charge of picking the gum off the ceiling since no one else wanted to do it. Ben asked us if he should stand on a wobbly desk to get the gum down off the ceiling. We all said yes just so we could finish cleaning faster, ignoring the dangers of it.

Ben quickly reassured us of the dangers. You could hear the worry in his voice. There was no point in moving the desks since the desks were cemented to the floor anyways.

"Just use it," the rest of us sighed out.

I decided to wipe off the teacher's desk in front of the chalkboard.

Julian was cleaning the chalkboard when he blew chalk dust all over me. "Oops," he said sarcastically, trying to act like it was an accident.

I grabbed a random water bottle next to the desk and poured it over Julian's head. Since there was only a little bit of water in the bottle the water soaked into by his thick hair and only little droplets got to his school uniform.

Trey started laughing hysterically at Julian and Julian pushed Trey, embarrassed that his plan had backfired on himself. Julian and Trey fought until they bumped into Jazmine and caused her to fly into me and accidentally push me into a desk. We heard a quiet yelp and then a loud thud behind us.

Ben lay lifeless on the floor.

We stood there for a little bit, shocked more than anything.

Trey ran up to the boy and checked his pulse. "Nothing," he said, indicating that Ben's heart had already stopped beating.

All we could do was stare. We couldn't make out our emotions. Was it fear? Sadness? Guilt? I'm not sure.

All of a sudden Jazmine started flat out balling. "We killed him," she cried.

"No, we didn't," Julian defended us.

"Yes, we did. He warned us the table was wobbly, but we just didn't listen!" she yelled back.

How were we supposed to know that he was going to fall?

"You guys shouldn't have been fighting!" I yelled.

"What are we gonna do?" Trey asked as water threatened to escape from his eyes.

"We're gonna have to turn ourselves in," Jazmine said bluntly.

"And go to jail? I think not!" Julian interjected.

"We just killed a boy!" Jazmine yelled, even more angry than before. "Besides, our parents will probably bail us out anyway!"

"No! All my athletic scholarships will be thrown in the trash!" Julian argued with a shaky voice.

"You probably won't even make it to become a football player. Your parents will force you to take over their company and won't let you achieve your dreams. They don't care about us. All they care about is their money!" Jazmine shouted.

"You guys are missing the point! We still have to figure out what we're gonna do!" I interjected.

"We need a cover up story," Trey said.

"What? This is crazy!" Jazmine replied.

"Any ideas?" I asked with my head down. I was so ashamed but not ashamed enough to go to jail.

"We can say we all went to take a bathroom break, but Ben decided to stay back," Julian suggested.

"And when we came back, we found him here on the ground," Trey continued.

"Who's gonna believe that?" Jazmine asked with a more worried look on her face now.

"There's four of us. If we all say the same thing, I'm sure they'll believe us," Julian said.

"Well, then let's call the police," I stated.

Two days later I got up to grab the mail. Me and the other kids involved in the incident got to stay home for a week after what happened. As I came back inside, I noticed a letter that read *To: Ms. Saige Kim*. I opened it and saw it was an invitation to Ben's funeral.

"Are you going to go?" My mom startled me as I realized she was still home.

"I don't know. I should, shouldn't I?"

"I don't think you should. They don't exactly like us." She paused. "Actually, I'd think they'd appreciate you taking the time to pay their son some respect. They did invite you after all so maybe there's no longer a grudge against us. But that situation must've been so traumatic for you. Are you ready to face *him* again?"

I nod my head. I think I should look past our family differences.

The next day was the day of the funeral. When I arrived, it started raining once again, setting the mood for this poor boy's death. Everyone stood circled around the casket with black umbrellas and dark jackets or coats. There was a hole right next to other gravestones that shared the same last name as Ben, and I guessed that's where he'd be buried. I couldn't help but look around to see if the others were there and they were. They seemed to wonder the same thing as we all looked up and stared at each other.

At the ceremony back at the Russo's home everyone was asked to turn our phones into a bin so no disruptions would be made during the speeches given.

I got startled by someone grabbing my wrist, but it turned out it was just Julian. He pulled me to the upstairs bathroom where nobody was. "Does this seem fishy to you?" he asked.

"What do you mean?"

"The Russo's invited all of us, but they hated us even before the incident."

"Julian, they've obviously had a change of heart. They took the time to invite us so that says something."

He nodded in agreement and we both headed back downstairs.

A few speeches were given and even a small shout out was given to the four of us for "Calling the police immediately and doing all that we could to help save him" even though that wasn't exactly the case.

And soon after, everyone started to leave one by one. The four of us took some extra time trying to find our phones since for some reason they were no longer in the bin. Thankfully, Ben's mother found our phones and handed them back to us.

I was very confused on why they weren't still in the bin in the first place.

Two days later and it was our first day back to school since the incident. We heard that the newly recruited teacher that had sentenced us all to detention was fired for endangering the life of a student. Although she did give us a dangerous task, I still felt bad that she had gotten the blame. Word seemed to spread fast, as everyone looked at me with pity. I pulled my gray hoodie over my head and tightened the strings so people wouldn't see my face. When I went to my locker I found cards and tiny trinkets inside that said stuff like *sorry for your loss* and *feel better soon*, even though I wasn't the one that should've been receiving those. Under all the junk there was a white piece of paper with my schedule on it that showed a schedule change. I read *how to cope with the loss of others*.

I passed Ben's locker and realized that there weren't any cards or messages in front of his locker even though he was the one that passed. How sad.

In the middle of class, I got a notification on my phone but I didn't pay attention to it and continued with my work.

Soon class was over. I headed to my locker where Jazmine stood already waiting for me. She quickly pulled me to an empty classroom where Julian and Trey were already waiting, and I couldn't help but notice the stares we received passing the other students. Both me and Jasmine were the last people you'd think you'd see together.

"What is it this time?" I asked.

"Did you get this message too?" Julian asked.

I took out my phone from my back pocket and read the message that I had gotten during my last class. ***You tried to cover up that poor boy's death, but you didn't cover it up from me!*** it read.

"How did they even get our numbers?" Julian asked.

"Someone else knows what really happened," Jazmine stated.

"How do you know that?" I asked, too scared to believe that it could be true. I blocked the number.

"Don't block it. We have to find out who it is!" Jazmine said worriedly.

"It's probably just some kid that's pranking us." I left the room, leaving the others behind dumbfounded.

The next period, I got another notification but this time I looked at it. ***Try blocking me again and it won't work. Instead, I'll just release the truth and you and your families will be looked down upon by society for lying and being selfish.*** The person messaging then sent surveillance videos of us fighting and knocking Ben over. I quickly got up and ran out of class.

Julian did the same.

The others ran to the room too, all panicking and worrying about what was going to happen.

"The security cameras," Trey whispered.

"Now we have to find out who it is." Jazmine glared at me.

"And what are we gonna do when we find them? Threaten them?" I asked.

"He probably wants money," Trey said.

I started texting them. *How much do you want?*

Not everything revolves around money. But I want the truth, if not from you then your parents.

The message left us a little confused.

"Our parents?" Jazmine asked.

We all seemed to rub the question off though.

"Who in the school has access to the security cameras?" Julian asked.

"The principle, the guards, and the janitors do," Trey replied.

"It must be one of them," Julian continued.

"Why didn't they go to the police already?" Trey asked.

"Let's find out," I suggested.

"How about we meet up at my place after school. I'll make a separate group chat for us and send you guys the address. We need to make a plan," Jazmine said.

We nodded our heads.

After school was over, we all met up at Jazmine's home, a big 3 story condo that was located at the top of one of our city's tallest buildings. There were huge windows in every room with big fancy curtains. Big crystal chandeliers hung from every ceiling and every piece of furniture was made from either silk or cashmere. She took us up to her rooftop where you could see the whole entire city.

"We break into the school," Julian stated.

"What?!" Trey exclaimed

"How?" I asked.

"What do you mean, how? There is no way we're breaking into that school," Trey said.

"You may not want to, but we will. I'll do whatever it takes to stop the world from knowing what actually happened," Jazmine simply said.

"Tell us a way to get into the school," I demanded from Trey.

He sighed. "The security cameras are shut off between the hours of 7:00 and 8:00 pm for them to reset. All you have to do is climb over the gate. The security cameras should be in the front office near the principal's room. But be careful of the security guard at the front gates."

"We should get going," Jazmine said.

"We're doing it now?" Julian asked.

"The sooner we get that surveillance the better chance no one else will find out," Jazmine said.

When we arrived, we hid across the street and tried to figure out how we'd get past the security guard. The security guard roamed only the front of the gates toward the streets. We had to go to the side of the school to break in. We quickly ran across the street and hopped the fence, then climbed through the front office window and grabbed the key from the bin. Jazmine opened the computer and was greeted to a screen that asked for a password.

"Here, I have an idea of what it could be," Julian said. He pushed Jazmine out the way.

"How?" Jazmine asked.

"Do you know how many times I've been here?" Julian said sarcastically. "Got it! But we need another code."

We didn't know what it was, so we split up in hopes of finding the password.

Jazmine and I made our way up to the storage room.

"Why is the doorknob broken?" I was confused. I knew I didn't go to the storage room much, but it definitely should not be broken.

"Maybe one of the staff broke it by accident." Jazmine shrugged.

Although that was a possibility, I thought someone had tried to find something, just like we were. We walked into the storage room and started looking under papers and notebooks.

"I got nothing," Jazmine said.

"I found this staff log. Maybe if it's someone who works here that knows what we did."

We left to see if Julian had found the passcode.

After making it back downstairs we heard footsteps behind us. We both quickly turned around only to find no one there.

"Julian?" I asked, making sure I wasn't just being delusional.

"Found it!" Julian shouts from behind us, scaring both me and Jazmine.

Back to the principal's office, we retrieved the surveillance cameras and headed back to Jazmine's place.

Everyone walked in one by one, and we all sat spread out from each other. The teacher walked in and sat down at his desk. He was my old health teacher back in freshman year and I was surprised he hadn't been fired by the number of times he let kids do whatever they wanted while he slept.

"So, I heard you guys recently witnessed the death of a boy who attended this school. We will be meditating and trying to dispose of all those feelings of sorrow." He turned on his speaker and started playing meditation music. "Everyone, close your eyes and take deep breaths. Then lay your back against the chair and relax."

We all knew he was just gonna fall asleep, so we gave each other looks, hinting that we were gonna skip the rest of class. We planned to go to the rooftop, but I decided to run to my locker and get a snack first. When I opened my locker, I noticed a folded piece of paper, but I threw it away assuming that it was just another sympathy card for Ben's death.

Once we got up to the rooftop, I slammed down the staff log that I had found in the storage room the night before. Trey and Julian gave me weird looks as I realized they weren't informed on why I had grabbed this.

"What is this for?" Julian asked, confused.

"You guys know how whoever is messaging us has the surveillance tape. How did they know where to find the surveillance tape if they don't work here?" I said.

"You're saying it could be one of the staff members?" Trey asked.

"Bingo," Jazmine said, answering his question for me.

"The number of staff that work here is huge though. There's no way we'll be able to find out who it is," Julian said.

"Not necessarily, we only have to look at the janitors, guards, and the principal since they are the only ones with clear access to the surveillance tapes," Trey explained.

"That's still a big selection of people," Julian said.

"Have any of you guys gotten into any conflicts with any of those people?" I asked everyone.

Julian started saying a list of people he had had conflicts with. And boy was that list long.

"Anyone else?" Jazmine sighed.

Everyone else shook their heads.

"Ugh, we're never going to find out who it is." Jazmine threw herself onto the ground.

Aww giving up already? Why? We're just getting started.

The four of us quickly sat up at the message.

"They can hear us?" Jazmine asked.

We all frantically looked at other buildings and around the rooftop.

There's no point in looking around, you'll never find me unless you turn yourselves in.

The same person messaged us.

Why are you doing this to us? I texted them.

I'm tired of you rich people acting so stuck up and thinking you can get away with everything. I figured, why not torture you guys. It seems fun, does it not?

Umm… no it doesn't. Look there has to be some other reason you're doing this. Jazmine texted.

Maybe. But you kids will have to find that out yourselves.

"What? This doesn't make sense!" Trey yelled.

The bell rang, implying that the last period was over and it was time to go. The four of us ran downstairs back into our classroom to grab all our things. I noticed a little droplet of blood on my desk table. I wiped it up with a tissue but threw it away without wondering where it came from. I then noticed another droplet on my shoes. Then another on the floor right next to me. Then another and another.

I finally realized where it was coming from. I looked up.

The words *You killed him* were written on the ceiling tiles in blood. I grabbed paper towels and climbed on my desk to wipe off the blood that was on the ceiling, not wanting anyone to see it.

Suddenly, I heard screws fall on the floor.

I looked down and noticed the screws from the desk chair were gone. I immediately lost my balance. Before I fell to the floor, Julian caught me, leaving me dumbfounded since it all happened too fast. As I got down from his arms, I realized that I could've gotten killed. All four of us looked up at each other and realized just how much danger we were in.

Fighting For Change
by Laila Butcher, Age 16

I have the right to be well cared for in my parent's absence.

September 22nd, 2007, my home in Elk Grove, CA.

This is where it all started. I was about three years old when my mom was taken away for good. I was sent into foster care, a place where no child should be, a scary place with no sense of familiarity or consistency, constantly moved from home to home. But fortunately, my grandma found me and took me out of the system, becoming my legal guardian. I've been with her since.

Summer July 2017, my mom sues my grandma for custody.

I was thirteen, weighing my options, getting second opinions but still couldn't decide whether I should start a new life, or continue the one I had. Do I pick up everything and leave or stay grounded where I'm at and figure the rest of my life out later. Things were moving too fast, and the system was putting unimaginable amounts of pressure on me when I could barely understand my situation. So, I stayed with my grandma, and this ended up being the best decision in the long run—but my relationship with my mom was now tainted, and there wasn't much I could do but wait for her to mature. When you're in prison your progression stops while the world around you keeps going. Adaptation is a real struggle that people such as my mom had to deal with when she was released. This caused a strain on our relationship for a few years, but now we are better than ever. She's done her own personal growing and healing, and so have I. Sometimes it feels as if she never left.

Present Day

I am fighting for change. I am taking my struggles and turning them into successes. I am helping build my community and showing other kids like me that their past doesn't define them. No matter what you go through in life there is always a bright side of things. I have changed a situation that incites pity into a story of resilience that is uplifting for everyone. I want to dedicate my future to helping children with lives like mine to see the empowerment in their stories so that they realize how strong they truly are and use that to their advantage in their everyday lives.

I do this by working with organizations such as Project Avary. Project Avary is a youth advocacy group that focuses on ways to begin healing the emotional and social wounds of being a CIP, a Child of an Incarcerated Parent.

I joined Project Avary when I was seven years old. Since July of 2018, I have been a Junior Counselor at Project Avary where I co-lead group discussions with youth ages seven to ten and participate in monthly outings (pre COVID-19) called "adventure days."

Adventure days are designed to create a safe space for all Project Avary members to bond, share their stories, begin healing, and have loads of fun!

I also roll with a group called Peacemakers. Peacemakers is a teen advocacy program under Project Avary. Peacemaker's youth leaders help give voice to the forgotten and overlooked needs of children who have an incarcerated parent. As a youth leader and the child of an incarcerated parent, a CIP, I have been visiting men's prisons throughout Northern California to share my story and my experiences during my mother's ten-year incarceration period. I lead restorative circles with the Men in Blue (incarcerated men) to discuss the struggles, challenges, and social stigmas that I have faced, as a CIP.

I take my leadership role very seriously in this incredible program, as it requires a high level of maturity, compassion, and an inordinate amount of understanding.

Last but not least, I am also currently working with Project WHAT. We raise awareness about the effects of parental incarceration on children. As a Peer Mentor, I plan and facilitate weekly meetings that include topics such as: local and state policy changes that affect CIP's, pandemic challenges with online school, food insecurities, lack of socialization outside of immediate family, and the emotional impact of not being allowed prison visits with their loved ones. I also contribute to the development of training content for law enforcement agencies, doctors, therapists, attorneys, and others whose work includes perspectives and decisions that affect the lives of young people with incarcerated parents.

Why was it me?
by Rowan Feldman, Age 13

The Guatemalan civil war started in 1960 and lasted until 1996. The war was about politics. Farmers and poor people rebelled against the government who was taking their land and their rights. Thousands of children were separated from their families and there was a massive amount of over 200,000 people killed. Some children were found by the military, and they were put up for adoption. Many of them never saw their families again. Between the 1990s and 2000s, tens of thousands of Guatemalan children were adopted into the United States and internationally. In 2007 stricter adoption laws were passed. No international adoptions have been allowed since.

This story is based on the war, my Guatemalan background, and my being adopted.

BOOM! There was a loud roar coming from outside which made Jacquelyn jolt up, sweating and breathing heavily. Thunderstorms were normal in Guatemala, and Jacquelyn was used to it, but this seemed different. After a few moments of silence, she closed her eyelids to go back to sleep. BOOM! There was another loud roar, and this time Jacquelyn didn't ignore it. Suddenly there was a scream. The sound she heard wasn't thunder, it was the sound of gunshots. Now Jacquelyn's husband and daughter, Adriana were up. Jacquelyn grabbed her baby and wrapped her in the *robozo* on her back. Her husband, Carlos, held their other daughter's hand, Adriana. They scurried quickly out of their hut and could already see people running into the jungle.

Jacquelyn started running as fast as she could with her baby on her back, Carlos and Adriana running fast beside her. She heard a woman call out her name for help. Jacquelyn looked back. The woman fell to the ground. Her body lay still, and she was no longer breathing. She was shot. Murdered. Murdered by the military. It felt as though Jacquelyn's heart had broken in two. She knew that the woman's voice was her mother's. It was her mother's body that lay on the ground. Lifeless. She wanted to stay, to stay with the one who loved her and raised her. But she had to run.

It started to rain. The rain poured down hard on their faces, blinded them, made people stumble, the villages fell out of fear, and thunder, mixing with the gunshots. The gunshots were frightening, making the crowd run faster, in all directions. Jacquelyn ran as fast as she possibly could with her worn-out *huaraches*. She tried not to listen to all the noise around her, the crowd of people from their village screaming and panting from running, and their footsteps pounding hard on the ground like a stampede of cattle. The village had heard of the military attacking other villages, burning them, and killing people. They didn't think it could happen to them. They hadn't been prepared for the war that was coming.

Children, men, and women were running away from the military and their gunshots. Some were shot and fell to the ground. But Jacquelyn was unable to help them. She had to save her baby. She ran into the jungle, away from the crowd of people from her village, hoping that the military wouldn't find her and her baby. She no longer saw Carlos or Adriana. Almost all her energy had left her body. She stopped to look back at her eleven-month-old baby girl wrapped on her back. I have to keep running, she told herself. She tried not to think of what happened to her older daughter, Adriana, and her husband, Carlos. Jacquelyn couldn't see anyone in the darkness of the night jungle. She told herself don't think about them now. You have to keep running for your baby. Please let them be okay, please. She ran, farther and deeper into the jungle. It was hard to run in the dark with all the roots of the trees and branches that had fallen on the ground. Jacquelyn ran until she could take no more. The noise was getting further and further away. She couldn't tell if it was the pouring water or sweat that covered her face.

Jacquelyn couldn't see anything around her. It was dark, pitch black. She didn't know where she was, or how long she'd been running and fleeing from her village. She didn't want to know, she didn't want to know how long she'd been apart from her sweet Adriana and Carlos.

When she was too tired to run any longer, she looked at her baby and thought about what might have happened to Adriana and Carlos. It made her continue to run. Jacquelyn had to find a place where she and her baby could rest, a place that was safe from all the destruction and terror. It was starting to get a bit lighter, and the rain wasn't pouring down as hard. Up ahead Jacquelyn could just barely get a glimpse of something. Rocks. She ran faster, knowing that she could crawl under the rocks for protection. Running, Jacquelyn tripped over one rock. Her left foot slammed into another. She cried in pain, her foot starting to bleed.

The baby began to cry. She'd been silent the whole time, and now both were finally letting all their pain and fear out. Jacquelyn was crying and she was so exhausted that she didn't notice that she had fallen asleep.

Jacquelyn woke up early. She could feel a cold breeze. The smell of earth was comforting. She didn't hear or see anyone. She hadn't had anything to drink and longed for water. She needed to find water. Jacquelyn needed to find water to feed her baby. Her feet hurt from running so much. Jacquelyn's left foot had a deep gash from her fall. Her huaraches were in worse condition. They were torn apart and had holes in almost every single part of the shoe. But she didn't want to hurt her feet more in case she had to run more, so she kept her huaraches on, and went to search for water, leaving her baby sound asleep.

She found a stream, just out of sight from where she and her baby had slept. Jacquelyn fell to her knees and gulped down all the water she could. Her throat stopped throbbing and she decided to take a rest putting her feet in the water, hoping it would help the pain and soreness. She sat there trying to let go of her worries and pain. After a few minutes, Jacquelyn headed back to where she knew her baby was waiting. But when she got there, her baby was gone! Her heart rate started to go up again, like the night before. She felt a lump forming in her throat, and it started to tighten. Maybe this wasn't the right spot she told herself, trying to calm down by inhaling and exhaling slowly.

But nothing was fine.

She searched everywhere where she thought her baby could possibly be. Her baby wasn't there. She wasn't anywhere. Her baby was lost. She was gone. She was the one person, the one thing keeping Jacquelyn going. Where could she be!? I've already lost my husband and other daughter, what can I possibly do now...? I've lost my daughter, my mother, my husband, and all that I had left was my baby...and now she's gone too.

Preschool

I was sitting on the colorful rainbow rug in the back of the room, playing with one of my friends, Liam, as we waited for our moms.

A few minutes later I looked up, after hearing familiar footsteps. I could see my mom's golden blonde hair blowing in the wind through the long row of windows. She entered through the door, and like always, said hello and had a conversation with my teacher, Zena. I ran over to my mom with joy. I knew that it was time to go home. I gave her a big hug as she picked me up off the ground.

"Can I go say goodbye to Liam?" I asked as she put me back down.

"Sure!"

I ran over to my friend, but he had a confused expression on his face. Instead of me saying goodbye, he spoke first and raised his finger.

He pointed right at my mom, and asked: "Is that your mom?"

"Yeah," I said, starting to get confused myself.

"Then why is she white, and you're not?"

I shrugged my shoulders in a response I always use for not knowing the answer to questions. "I don't know."

Liam's face seemed even more bewildered than it was previously, but before he could say anything else, my mom came over and we walked out of the building.

"Mommy?"

"Yes, sweetheart?"

"Why are you and daddy white and I'm not?"

My mom's smile turned into her serious-looking face. She seemed to be trying to figure out what to say to me. We had talked about this many times, but I still felt confused. Finally, she looked at me. "You already know. It's because I didn't give birth to you. Another woman, your "birthmother" gave birth to you. But she couldn't take care of you, or so she thought, so she gave you up for adoption."

I was confused. I never really understood what my mom was saying, even though I had heard this before. "You mean I have another mom?" I asked.

"Yes. You are lucky, you know you have three moms: your birth mother Elvira, your foster mom Rosa Lydia, and your forever mom, that's me."

We continued to exit my preschool and were halfway home when I said: "I don't like how my skin color is different than yours!" I started to throw a tantrum. I stomped my foot on the ground. "I wish I could rip my skin off so I could have the same skin color as you."

My mom's face changed. She looked sad. She picked me up and held me close. She wanted to comfort me, but I wanted nothing of it. She didn't understand what it was like to have people staring at you when your mom was picking you up from school. She didn't understand that people looked at me and pointed at me. They all looked at me in a way that my mom couldn't understand. Because my dad was older than my mom people would ask me if my dad was my grandpa. My dad was my dad, but it would be something that my mom would never be able to understand. I wish that they could understand, but it was something that I felt I could understand.

Elementary School

"How was your first day at your new school?" my mom asked me as we walked our final steps to the car.

"It was okay."

"Are you and Anna in the same class?"

Anna was my best friend from preschool, and I had hoped she'd be in my class. We were the only ones from my preschool going to Harriet Tubman Elementary.

"No, she wasn't in my class," I said with a sigh.

"Aw, that's a bummer."

"Yeah. Mom?"

"Yes?"

"Why don't I have the same skin color as you?"

"It's because you're adopted, I didn't give birth to you...."

My ears stopped listening to my mom's words and a memory came into my mind. Back when I was in preschool, my mom had said the same thing to me then, back to before preschool when I was told the same thing.

"Your birth mother lives in Guatemala. She has beautiful mocha skin just like you. Do you remember a few years ago when you were in preschool that we talked about it?"

"Yeah... A little bit."

"Why are you asking about it now?"

"Cause a boy asked me why you were white and why I'm not when you came to pick me up."

I didn't tell my mom the full truth. A girl I met had also asked me why I was Guatemalan but didn't know how to speak Spanish. "I don't know," I had told her. The girl had looked at me and then started teasing me by speaking Spanish right in front of me so I wouldn't know what she was saying.

"Mom?"

"Yes?"

"Do you think I have a sister or brother?"

"I think you do have a sister. I'm not sure if you have a brother, but you have a sister."

I hadn't been expecting my mom to say that I had a sister, but as soon as I heard the words come out of her mouth my head turned and I was filled with excitement. "Really?"

"Yeah, I've been told that you have an older sister, Adriana."

The next day at school a boy had asked me why my skin color was different from my mom's skin color.

"I'm adopted," I said, knowing that he wouldn't understand the meaning of it.

"That's just kinda sad," he said after I explained what being adopted meant. "And if you have a sister, then why did they keep her and give you up?"

I didn't expect a question like this to pop into the conversation. "I—I don't know," I said, trying to shrug it off like it was nothing. I hadn't expected someone to ever ask anything like that. I felt so much weight on my shoulders. If I did have a sister, then why didn't my mom give her up too? Did she love me less than she did my sister? Did I do something wrong to make her love me less? Why did she give me up?

The Incident

"Hmm what do you think we need?" my mom asked as we strolled through the grocery store looking at a row of beverages.

"More special *agua*!" I said brightly. "Special agua" meant soda water, but we preferred to call it "special agua." I, my mom, and dad all drank a massive amount of it, and brought several bottles of it home.

"Hello!" An elderly woman with white and gray hair was behind us. "What a beautiful little girl you have! I bet she was expensive. How much did you pay for her?" She pointed at me, just like Liam had pointed at my mom when she was picking me up from preschool.

My mom's face turned bright red and she bit her lip as if to not let any words out her mouth. She looked at me and said quietly: "Let's go, honey, we have to get home soon so we don't miss dinner." She abruptly pushed herself past the woman and grabbed my hand leading us to the cashier.

Mom didn't say much and only talked with the cashier, who helped us check out.

We put all our groceries into the trunk of our car. "Mom? Why—what—why did the woman say that...?" I asked.

We climbed into the car.

My mom sat and took a deep breath in and exhaled out. She continued to sit, not starting the car. Finally, she said: "We don't look like most families. It confuses people sometimes. People can be curious about us or mean. That woman probably didn't mean to be rude, but it was rude of her to say that, and that's why I didn't respond to her. The most important thing is that we remember that we are all a family, and we love each other very much."

We both hugged. But I couldn't stop thinking about how "different" our family was compared to all of my friends and their families.

The Search

"Hey mom...do you think I'll ever meet my birth sister?"

My mom took a deep breath in as we carried our groceries up our stairs leading to the front door.

"We can certainly try and search for her, but I am not sure if we will find her. But we can try."

"Really?" I said in an astonished tone. My face brightened. I was so excited and happy that I almost dropped the bag of groceries that were in my hands.

"We will find a mother-searcher. It could take months, maybe longer," my mom said very seriously.

After my mom put the groceries away, she got on her computer and began asking our friends from our Guat Adopt group if they could recommend a searcher. I hadn't known that the Guatemalan group was a group of people who were also Guatemalan adoptees until my mom told me I was adopted. We had been to many gatherings together since I was very young. But it was something I did not enjoy in the least bit. I didn't know anyone, and I was extremely shy. Some of the girls would just point at me and laugh. I didn't understand why and always felt alone.

I remember hiding from everyone once and sitting behind a tree while I talked to myself. I didn't have any friends as everyone else did. No one was my age. I remember being the youngest. But most of all I remember being alone.

Around seven months later, the searcher that my mom had hired found my birth mom. We found out that I even had a younger brother, and that my birth mother had a boyfriend. I had always longed for a sister, and I badly wanted to meet her. A lot of the time, I felt lonely. My dad felt lonely sometimes too, we always called it "the lonely feeling." My friends usually kept me company, but at home, I felt alone.

Meeting my Birth Family

I didn't think that it would be as complicated as it was to meet my birth family. We had to take two airplanes, one to Houston, Texas, and then another plane to Guatemala City. Usually, I didn't like to travel, but I was so excited that I was sure that everyone on the plane could feel my enthusiasm. It was a bright sunny day and once we got off the plane and stepped foot in Guatemala, it started to get even hotter.

Guatemala wasn't anything like I pictured it. It was different from the home I was used to. Many people lived on the streets, which made me feel suddenly so lucky, but it also made me wonder why was I the one who was adopted...?

We took a long car ride from Guatemala City all the way to Huehuetenango. On our car ride there, our translator was with us, and she played games with me for the long six-hour drive.

Later, my nerves got to me. My mom and I were sitting in the lobby of the hotel, which had massive glass front windows. We should be able to see when my birth family arrived. I had to draw to try and distract myself from how scared, excited, and nervous I was. I put all my emotions, the happy, the excited, the nervous, and the scared ones into the colors of my bird drawing. I tried not to think about anything that would make me excited or scared, and just drew.

When I didn't want to draw any longer, I'd look up and wait to see a woman and a little girl like me, walking towards the entrance of the hotel. After many tries, I did see a woman and a little girl like me. They were both dressed in a very unique fabric that was unrecognizable to me. My mom got up from the seat that she had been sitting in while trying to calm me down and distract me with drawing.

The little girl and woman came closer, and closer, as we walked closer to them. I looked at my sister, her face looked somewhat like me, but with long black hair. Only her nose and hair looked different from mine. My hair was cut short, in a bob which my sister loved. I never liked it and had always wanted long hair like hers. She smiled. I wondered if she had ever wanted a sister too.

After introducing ourselves, and staring at each other for a while, and trying to talk, we all went to see some Mayan ruins that were nearby. They were big and looked like pyramids from Egypt that I'd seen in pictures. My sister and I started climbing the ones closest to us... They were massive. It was scary to look down when we got to the top.

My birth mom hugged me and kissed me so much. She seemed very relieved. I didn't know what she was saying, but she kept saying something. Even though she was my "real" mom, it was a bit weird to have her hugging me, and only just meeting her... But I was happy to see her.

I was most excited to see my sister, Adriana. Even though we could not speak the same language, we still had a connection. We used hand motions to somewhat talk. When my sister had to throw our little brother's diapers away, she looked at me and made a face of "this smells horrible." We both laughed like crazy.

The one unexpected part of our visit was that my birth mom didn't know how to speak Spanish. She spoke a language called "Mam," which was a Mayan language. We had brought a Spanish translator, but since my birth mom didn't know how to speak Spanish our conversations were a lot harder than we thought they would be. Usually, it started like this: my adoptive dad would say something, ask my adoptive mom if it was okay, she'd nod while crying and then the translator would say it to my birth mom's boyfriend in Spanish. Finally, my birth mom's boyfriend would say it to my birth mom who was also crying. Then it'd go back all the way around, and my parents would have to explain the conversation to me.

I learned that my birth mom didn't give me up for adoption. She lost me in the jungle. She had searched and searched for hours and hours for me. But she couldn't find me and thought she'd never see me again. I learned that my birth dad had left my mom to go and look for work, and never came back. It hurt. It was painful to know the truth. It stung. But it was good to know that I was loved and cared for by my birth mom and that she and Adriana were reunited.

There was a local craft market, which we headed to. My birth mom bought matching friendship bracelets for me and my sister. My sister would just smile all the time, and it was so fun to be with her, even though we couldn't speak the same language. My nervousness soon faded away, and I felt much better. My brother, David who was around two years old and still in diapers, was playing with a crocheted ball with his small hands, and he was laughing. We went to go ride horses, which was both a good and somewhat bad idea. My birth mom's boyfriend seemed to be terrified of the horses. However, my sister and my birth mom both had big smiles on their faces. Afterward, we all hugged. Both of my moms had tears in their eyes but smiled. And we headed home.

Five years later...

Five years. Five long years. I was almost ten and I hadn't seen my birth family in five long years. Now I was visiting them for the second time. However, this time I was gonna meet them at their house. I was more nervous this time, my hair had changed from the last time and was now flowing. This time I wasn't wearing a skirt like last time, but a tie-dyed shirt and blue pants. What made me so nervous this time was everything. I also had found out that my birth mom had gotten married to her boyfriend.

It was the same as last time. A stressful plane ride and a long six hours or so in the car driving up to where my birth mom lived.

When we got there, we could see a tiny house, about ten by twelve feet. On the right side of the house, there were tiny coops for hens and little cages. There were even two dogs who barked and snarled a bit as we walked over to the house.

My sister looked almost exactly the same as she did last time, just a bit older and mature. My younger brother David had grown up and looked like my birth mom's boyfriend. We all hugged as we saw each other. And my birth mom showed us a tour of her house.

Eventually, we heard little "peep, peeps" coming from somewhere.

My mom asked "*Donde esta peep peep?*", which meant "where is the sound peep peep coming from?"

My birth mom smiled. She brought us into her tiny house. There was a little basket with a bundle of cloth wrapped around it and on top of it. My mom took the tiny bit of cloth that was on the top and revealed... tiny chicks! They peeped and looked up at us. We all knelt down to pet them. I didn't notice, but my sister had slipped out of the room and went to go and get her pet bunny. The bunny was soft and a light pale brown. My sister put it into my arms and let me pet it.

This time we didn't go anywhere. We stayed at my birth mom's house. And this time, we had brought them presents. Clothes, school supplies, and some art supplies. This time, my mom knew how to speak Spanish. My sister, Adriana, could also speak Spanish.

I don't remember how long I stayed at their house, but what I do remember is that it was something that I'd always remember and keep in my heart. It was a special moment for all of us.

So many times, I had wished that I wasn't adopted so people wouldn't say to me how weird or sad it was to be adopted. I didn't want people to look and stare at me and point. I didn't like having a different skin color than my parents. I didn't want to look different and stand out in a crowd. I didn't want people to ask me why my parents were so far apart in age. I didn't want people to call my dad my grandpa. I didn't want to tell people the answers and have them reply "that's just sad" because it wasn't.

I've learned that it isn't sad that the universe brought me to my adoptive mom and dad. As I grew up, I realized that it is not sad that I am in America where I have all my friends who love and accept me for who I am. Nothing about it is sad. But through all of the worries, and all of the judgments, I've grown and I'm happy and proud. People can talk about me being different from my family members as much as they want, they can judge me, but I will always be proud that I'm adopted. I will always be proud to be raised by my adoptive mom and dad. No matter your skin color, race, or what you look like, be proud of who you are and stand tall.

It took me a long time to learn how to accept myself for who I am, but I'm proud of who I am. And I am proud of being adopted. And I will always be proud of all those parts of me.

The villagers

They could hear the soft cries of a baby. Barely. It was a faint cry, but nearby. The villagers rushed over to the noise, trying to figure out where a baby might be.

"Over here!" whispered one of the villagers. She picked the baby up and held her tightly.

"Where do you think the baby came from?" another villager whispered.

"I'm not sure...her parents could have left her there to try and protect her from the gunshots," the woman who was holding the baby said quietly.

Crack.

"Soldiers are coming!"

The woman with the baby in her arms and the rest of the villagers quickly ran away from danger and disappeared into the jungle.

The Truth Behind a Mask
by Giselle Caban, Age 15

Mariana

The Start of Something New - Blog Post 1
Mental health is a topic many people shy away from, but not me. Hi! I'm Mariana Vasquez and my goal is to spread awareness about mental health. Growing up was always hard for me and I always felt like an outsider. I didn't come from money like the other people in my school did, but I made it work. I work as a receptionist at a magazine company and I'm hoping to become a writer soon. So this is day one! I'm now gonna take you all around on this blog and help you realize it's okay to not be okay. Mental health matters.

Wearing a mask - Blog Post 2
I see people all around who look so happy, but I can't help but think about if they really are okay. I think they are just wearing a mask to hide their true feelings. Being transparent is hard, but just try. You don't always need to disguise the way you're feeling. Be real! Be you! I'm always here if you need to talk! - Mariana

Brrrring! Brrring! Mariana reached up from the pile of blankets that covered her body. She flopped her hand around her dresser, wrestling to turn off the alarm. Today, something felt different. After a long game of five more minutes, she finally got up to brew her morning coffee. She walked around her small dirty studio apartment with her coffee and laptop in her hand trying to make room to sit. Everywhere was cluttered with clothes or hair where Lola, her dog, had taken over. She threw her laundry onto her other existing piles of clothes on the floor when *ding*!

She jumped up for her phone. It was a reminder to take her new medication which she always forgot to do. For some reason, she was hoping for something else when her phone buzzed again. Another *ding* followed right away. She reread the text several times to make sure she wasn't hallucinating.

Dear Mariana Vasquez, I've read your manuscript and find it promising. I'd like for you to come in so we can chat.

Mariana screeched in excitement. "Lola! Lola! Oh my god! A publisher is interested in my manuscript!" The excitement quickly faded and instead a rush of sadness replaced it. The only person she could confide in was her dog. After pushing away all her friends and family for her relationship, things got lonely, especially once Gabriel was gone from her life.

Natalia

"Oh my god! I'm late! No, not today. Please not today," Natalia screamed to herself aloud. She jumped out of bed and ran through her lavishly modern and spotlessly clean apartment. So as not to seem too sterile, she'd picked mauve pillows for her minimalistic white couch and a cream throw blanket.

She jumped into the shower as fast as she possibly could and took special care to not wet her hair, hoping some dry shampoo would do the trick. After jumping out, she rummaged through her neat, color-coordinated closet in a towel looking for something professional to wear to court. She threw on some black slacks and paired a white turtleneck with a black blazer and finished the look with black heels. As basic as the outfit was, her tall curvy figure filled out the ensemble perfectly.

Natalia always stood out in a crowded room with the beauty of Aphrodite, but she didn't know it. She sprinted out of her apartment, grabbing her keys and phone with her makeup, laptop, and case files along the way. There was just enough time to grab some coffee before court.

"Natalia! What took you so long? You're lucky your clients aren't here yet," Stacey snapped. Stacey Brownfield has been Natalia's best friend in the whole wide world since they met in fifth grade. Stacey also happened to be Natalia's assistant. When Natalia explained her interest in wanting an assistant, Stacey had been job hunting for months, so she was pleased to help her friend and get some experience in law. Stacey always had a positive and uplifting effect on Natalia's mood.

"I'm so sorry, Stace! I missed my alarm, ran to grab a coffee on the way and then had the weirdest encounter at the shop. But I did bring you your favorite coffee and scone."

"Well Nat, tell me the story later because the trial is about to start. Thanks for the treats though!" Stacey replied.

They rushed off into court and Natalia downed her coffee before her clients showed up. As one of the top immigration lawyers in all of New York, her days were always busy.

"We can head to lunch now since you don't have another meeting until two and you can tell me about this *mysterious* meeting this morning," Stacey said after the trial.

They walked out of a skyscraper that looked as if its top was touching the sky. The panels of the building were so bright and clean that the light bounced off each window similar to the way a diamond catches the light. The wind blew in their faces as the door opened.

"It was just so weird, Stace. I walk into the coffee shop and the girl before me is having the hardest time picking what to order. Since I was in a rush, I kindly offered her a suggestion. When she turned to look at me, she didn't look well. She looked like she got no sleep last night and her makeup from the night before was still on."

"Oh my god. Did you talk to her?" Stacey interrupted.

"Don't interrupt me, that's rude," Natalia jokingly snapped. "The girl says 'you look so familiar. I feel like I've seen you before.' And I reply, sorry, maybe you've got the wrong person because I've never seen you before. After that she just obsesses on trying to figure out the connection. She was not letting go of the fact that I looked so familiar. She just kept pestering me and asking me all these questions. I told her I was just trying to get a coffee and I was super late, so I ran off."

"That's so weird. I'm glad you got away from her, that sounded like such a weird situation. Also, I'm freezing. I forgot my coat. We need to go back," Stacey said.

"I'll wait outside, Stace, hurry back." Natalia yelled, as Stacey was almost a hundred yards away already. She quickly pulled out her phone while waiting for her to return and opened her social media. She typed: *Gabriel Martinez*. His account instantly popped up with a new picture which she *obviously* clicked on. "Sixty-four comments! He usually only gets ten at most!" As she clicked on the comments, she felt a shove from behind that sent her phone flying out of her hands. She ran as fast as she could to catch it.

"Oh my god! I am so sorry. It's just been a hectic day and I haven't been on this side of town so I'm trying my best to not be late for my new..."

The familiar voice was instantly cut off as Natalia screamed "no" realizing the damage that has been done.

"Oh my god! Did I crack it? I can repay you."

Natalia hadn't cracked her phone. The damage was much worse. She accidentally liked her ex-boyfriend's picture! Still in shock, Natalia forced words out while she still stared at her phone. "Don't—don't worry it's nothing," she said. "Sorry, I just overreacted." She looked up to realize this was the woman of her strange interaction from the coffee shop earlier.

"This has to be fate or something," the coffee shop girl burst out. "I knew I had seen you somewhere before and now I'm running into you again. So sorry about your phone, let me see the damage." As the woman looked over Natalia's shoulder at the damage, her face turned to instant shock. "Oh my god," she gasped. Her tan skin went pale. She apologized and quickly ran away with tears swelling her eyes and not another word as if she had seen a ghost.

Natalia looked around confused, trying to piece together why this woman she kept bumping into ran off in such a hurry and without explanation. "Stacey, did you see that?" she exclaimed.

"Yes, let me guess… that was weird coffee shop girl," Stacey said, reading Natalia's mind as if they were the same person.

They walked off to get lunch, still rehashing the mysterious interaction.

Mariana

Panic Attacks in Public - Blog Post 3
Life gets hard sometimes, and we all have triggers. For me it's seeing specific things, people, or just reminders of a person that used

to be in my life. You just need to remember to breathe and know that you're safe. Do whatever is best for you. Go to a safe place and just stay there until you're better.

Much love,
Mari

After the confusing interaction, Mariana ran down the busy street, avoiding the other pedestrians around her. The tears kept running down her face as she struggled to catch her breath. Her chest heaved up and down. She ran into the nearest shop and asked to use the restroom to clean herself up. *Just let it all out. You'll feel better after. It's okay.* She reminded herself of the email she received earlier to chat about her manuscript and hopefully even get it published. It was such good news! She had to be focused today.

She watched herself in the mirror and tried to calm her breathing and stop shaking, but her tears continued to stream uncontrollably down her face. She had taken off her invisible mask to show her true feelings.

She used her tips from therapy to help calm herself. *Tapping.* She tapped her fingers along the side of her hand where her pinky was, then she switched hands, next she tapped on her forehead, then her cheekbones, her chin, her heart, and lastly her shoulders. This helped to soothe her anxiety and she did it constantly when the medication seemed like it wasn't helping.

After she felt better, she made herself presentable again to meet the new publisher and wrote something short to publish on her blog.

On the way out, she bought earrings to make up for taking up the store's bathroom for so long. Her mask was back on as she was able to push down her feelings and walk out of the store, head held high and ready to sell her book.

"What do you mean you're not going to publish my manuscript? I thought the whole point of me coming here was for you to work out edits and publishing contracts," Mariana shouted, struggling to keep her professional composure. "I worked so hard on this!"

The publisher looked at her with a face she couldn't read. "Look, Ms. Vasquez, you are a very talented writer, but my email was to meet and discuss your promising work so I could help you." The publisher paused trying to find the right words before continuing. "To be quite honest, I had a friend ask me to work with you and this is me returning the favor. I just don't think your manuscript is there. You need to add more to the story, flesh out the characters and plot. Like when Gabriella finds out her boyfriend has been cheating on her the whole time. You need a big moment for the reader," he concluded.

Mariana sat shocked, not understanding what he meant by a friend asking him to meet with her. *I'm probably just overanalyzing*. He was trying to help, but she didn't like his ideas. "A moment?" she questioned.

"You need to add more depth to your character. You can't try and have a strong female protagonist when she is anything but strong. She's really just, well—female. Blow me away. Then maybe we can talk about publishing this."

Anything but strong? How could he even say that? This character is based on me. "Look, Mr. um publisher sir," she proclaimed, ready to tell him off. "I will take this into consideration and get back to you," she replied, on second thought. Discouraged, Mariana told the man she understood.

Mariana exited the building to the New York sidewalk. She felt small surrounded by tall skyscrapers as she continually replayed the meeting inside her head. *Maybe he was right. I should've said more.* She thought that picking herself up and throwing herself into therapy had made her strong, but it seemed as if it would have been better for her to tell Gabriel off. He had cheated on her for years without her knowing and she just walked away as if nothing had happened. The other girl was very pretty though, but so was Mariana or at least people told her she was. She still couldn't help but question why she wasn't enough for him. Meandering the downtown streets with everything swirling in her head, she looked up and she saw *her* again.

Natalia

"Uh oh! 12 o'clock, stalker coming towards us," Stacey joked as they walked back from lunch. Natalia looked up and whispered to Stacey that she finally felt like she knew this woman from somewhere but couldn't place her as she approached them. The woman sped up to them stopping them in their tracks.

"It's you! You're the one Gabriel cheated on me with! You're Natalia," the woman wept.

That's where Natalia knew her from and why this girl freaked out earlier when she saw her phone. Fate had brought them together, but why? She felt badly seeing tears streaming down the woman's face.

"Oh my god, you're Mariana," Natalia said. *Don't cry. People will start to question you.*

They stood in shock for what felt like an eternity until Stacey apologized to Mariana.

"Hey, I'm sorry to break this up, but we don't have time. We have to go!" She pulled Natalia by the arm to move her along.

Natalia looked back at Mariana trying to apologize for them having to leave.

Mariana

Not again. I can't cry anymore. This needs to stop! Mariana always tried to be outwardly strong, but she was *very* emotional. She suffered from anxiety and depression, and she didn't know how to be okay with her mental illnesses without feeling like something was wrong with her. She had started the blog hoping it could help her and others see that you don't always have to pretend to be okay when you're not. Her mental illnesses were something she learned to deal with and at times even conquer while dealing with so much. She had many different ways to soothe herself like breathing, tapping, and even the 5-4-3-2-1 technique. When her anxiety would start to act up, she would focus on five things she could see, four things she could touch, three things she could hear, two things to smell, and one thing she could taste. This helped her focus on something else and relieve the stress.

After Gabriel, none of her techniques could help her.

After Gabriel, her whole world came crashing down.

He had made her feel loved at the beginning of their relationship until they started to have fights almost every day. Then one night the fighting got worse. He had become distant and was out working all the time. Mariana had pieced it together while lying awake waiting for him to come home. In her late-night delirium she would over-analyze every little thing. That this was when he had started to hang out with Natalia, she just knew it. Mariana had been suspicious all along, and when Gabriel came home late one night, she was furious.

"Gabriel!" She yelled his name with fury. "I know you've been out. You reek of alcohol! Please, Gabriel, tell me where you've been. This isn't you." She pleaded for him to talk to her. He had stormed away into the bedroom, slamming the door behind him without answering Mariana's questions. She had dropped to the floor and held herself, allowing herself to cry it all out. Bottling up her feelings never worked for her. This was when Mariana had realized this wasn't the guy she fell in love with.

Natalia

While the smell of vanilla hung in the air from their candle burning, Natalia and Stacey plopped themselves onto the couch with ice creams in their hands and eyes glued to the TV. Piles of crumpled tissues were all around them and new boxes close by, only to be grabbed on numerous occasions. Rachel McAdams cried the words, 'You wrote me,' as rain drenched the couple. Just like the rain in the movie, Stacey had tears streaming down her face. She looked over to see that Natalia wasn't crying.

"I don't want to cry, because if I do, it will be over Gabriel and not the movie," Natalia explained.

"Nat, are you serious? Crying over someone does not make you any less strong! No matter how badly you don't want to think about it, you found this great guy, so you quickly fell in love with him. You were together for some time when you found out the entire time he had a separate girlfriend! You can't possibly want him back. Don't you remember him chasing after you for months and you told me 'Stacey if I ever think of going back to that jerk please slap me, please knock some sense into me'." Stacey sniffled through tears from the movie.

As much as Natalia wanted to be strong, she knew in her heart that all her tears would come out eventually. The problem was, she wasn't the type to be sad in front of people. Natalia was one who buried herself in her work and processed her emotions in private.

"I did a thing," she said, knowing this could backfire. "When I walked off to the bathroom, I texted Mariana. I apologized for how we left and told her that I was hoping we could meet up to talk about our overlapping situation." She was nervous to see what Stacey would say, expecting her to say it was a bad idea.

"I think that was a really good move. You guys can talk about Gabriel and everything that happened and maybe become friends," Stacey stated optimistically.

They smiled at each other happily since they both agreed.

"Let's see if she responded. Hopefully, I didn't get rejec..." But before she could finish her sentence, complete shock flew across her face. She was as pale as a ghost. "I think I'm gonna be sick." Natalia threw her phone and ran to the bathroom throwing up everything she had left in her body.

Stacey ran to the phone to see what the big fuss was about. She threw the phone so high that it touched the ceiling while she screamed, "No!"

Mariana

Things were never the same after that first big fight. From then on, they were constantly fighting and even bickered about the small things. Mariana felt in her heart that he was being unfaithful to her, but every time it was brought up, he would find ways to flip it on her. She pushed through her discomfort of sharing her feelings and would ask him about the numerous girls she was suspicious of, only to have him debunk every one. The more suspicious she got and the more arguing, the less Gabriel was around. He was an expert at twisting her words. "So now I'm a bad boyfriend because I went out with my friends *one* time," Gabriel had mocked with sarcasm dripping from his voice during the night of their big fight.

"Gabe, it's not just one time and I never said you were a bad boyfriend. I just don't see you anymore," Mariana pleaded, with a weak attempt to hide the pain in her voice. She thought she could be herself with Gabriel, but now she was walking on eggshells around him.

One day, after a string of fights and not seeing Gabriel for days, she took a walk along the beautiful streets of New York to enjoy the fresh air and get some coffee. As she walked into the nearest coffee shop, her heart skipped a beat as she felt a lump rise in her throat. There he was, Gabriel, who she hadn't seen in days since their last blowup! Gabriel was holding hands with another woman. He looked nervous and kept looking around as if he was trying to hide from someone, which he was. How stupid could he be taking a woman to our neighborhood coffee shop? He was always so cocky. He thought he was better than everyone.

The woman turned around and saw Mariana. Mariana had tears in her eyes while she watched the couple. Confused, the woman looked back at Gabriel, then back at Mariana again. He said something to her, and she said something back, but Mariana couldn't make out the words because of the distance. Gabriel suddenly looked angry.

Mariana rushed out before she could make a scene, but as she turned to leave, she looked back just in time to see the woman place a hard slap across Gabriel's face. Mariana took a deep breath in and dropped her shoulders. She left the scene with an ache in her heart and walked home in defeat. Once she was home, she started packing up Gabriel's things. One by one she neatly packed up each of his belongings. She left the suitcase out the front door, then got in her car, making sure she wasn't home by the time Gabriel got there. The silence was almost deafening. She wasn't sure where she was going, but she couldn't stop. She had to keep moving.

Gabriel had cheated on her, but for how long? With whom? Was she not pretty enough? And while she was fighting for their relationship, he had a separate girlfriend behind her back, was there something she did to cause this? Something she didn't do? She couldn't help but feel stupid for trusting him and not going with her gut in the first place.

She took all her pain and sorrow from that relationship to write her story only to be rejected by a publisher that told her that her character wasn't strong enough. After seeing Natalia, she was inspired to write. She rewrote her book and made sure it was her best work.

Ding!

She was too in the zone to grab her phone to check who it was. Later, when she felt like it she'd check.

Natalia

After Natalia's extreme reaction to the message subsided, she ran back to her phone, snatched it from Stacey's hand, and was ready to respond.

"Nat, you have got to be kidding me! You're not actually thinking of responding?" Stacey questioned her furiously. "He cheated on you! He had another girlfriend throughout your entire relationship." She looked back at Natalia expecting her to agree and say she wouldn't respond.

Natalia ignored Stacey and reread Gabriel's message. *Hey Nat, I hope you're doing okay. I've been thinking about you and when I saw you like my picture, I took that as my opening. I miss you Nat and I know what I did to you was terrible, but I'm hoping you can forgive me. We had something good, I don't want to let it go to waste.*

"Nat, are you serious? I saw you completely depressed after what happened. All you did was work and when you weren't working you were sleeping or in a daze and I couldn't even get you to say a word to me." Stacey was not only furious, but worried for her friend. She didn't want to see her friend get hurt again.

Natalia started to type, and Stacey picked up her things to leave. "I can't believe you right now," she yelled as she slammed the door leaving Natalia alone.

Mariana

"Come on, Lola," Mariana called out so Lola would come to lay with her. As soon as Lola came to lie down Mariana turned over and took out her phone to check her notifications. *No. Please, I can't deal with this right now.* She read the message aloud a few times to make sure she wasn't dreaming. *Hey Mari, how did it go with your publisher?*

How did Gabriel even know about that? She questioned in her mind how he knew. Immediately, as if he could hear her thoughts, he responded. *I know this is gonna sound crazy, but I got you that meeting.* Mariana's heart shattered at the thought that he could be telling the truth. She was done with Gabriel. He couldn't cause her any more pain, and now this? This shot at her career was giving her so much hope and happiness, but he was supposedly responsible for it? *Mari, you know I loved you and I still do. I'm sorry for what I did, I was just going through something, but I'm here now. I want to make us work and help you reach your dreams, Mari, I miss you.*

After everything he put her through, he still found a way to get under her skin. All of a sudden, he was calling her nonstop. No matter how many times she declined, he wouldn't stop calling and texting. *Meet me. Tomorrow. Coffee shop.* And with that, she lay awake for hours, thinking of how bad of an idea it would be if she actually showed up.

Natalia

"Like I've said a million times before, let me make my own decisions. I'm going to meet him no matter what you say," Natalia said angrily.

Stacey had been trying to convince Natalia to not talk to him, but the second he asked to meet up, she fell for his tricks all over again.

Ding.

"Oh, it's Mariana," Natalia said, shocked that she even responded to her message. "She says that we should meet up tomorrow." Immediately Natalia felt stressed. How was she supposed to meet with Mariana *and* Gabriel?

"Tell Mariana that you can meet her at the coffee shop after you meet with Gabriel," Stacey said, trying to help Natalia.

Natalia agreed with her saying it was a good idea.

The next day, they woke up early. Stacey spent the night helping Natalia get ready by picking out the perfect outfit. She needed to be ready to see the guy who broke her heart and made her feel like she needed to put on this mask. The clothes she wore were a part of her mask, they helped her hide how much he had hurt her. She wouldn't show how she had fallen into a depression. As she was putting on the finishing touches, she reminded herself, *she was Natalia Vega. A very successful immigration lawyer. One of the best in her field. She was strong and wouldn't let one guy bring her down so low.*

When she was done getting ready, she grabbed her things and ran out of the house. She was ready to meet with Gabriel. Natalia didn't feel one speck of nervousness until the moment she pulled up. As she walked up to the coffee shop and was about to open the door, she looked up to see *them*.

Mariana

"Gabriel, stop. You cheated on me and now you think you can just walk into my life again. It's not fair," Mariana said. She avoided eye contact with him.

"Mari please, I'm sorry for what I did to you," Gabriel said. He reached for Mariana's hand.

The touch of his hand shocked Mariana causing her to try and pull away, but he held on tight. Slowly she looked up at him, his beautiful brown eyes pierced into her soul and she thought she saw a familiar face, but then no, this was not a familiar person. He wasn't the kind and sweet Gabriel who she had fallen in love with. He was a completely different person now with manipulation and dishonesty in his eyes.

A cold breeze flew in from the door opening and awoke her from her daze. She looked up to see Natalia standing in the doorway looking almost as heartbroken as the day Mariana walked in on Natalia and Gabriel in this very same coffee shop.

"Oh shoot," Gabriel said as Mariana quickly took her hand back from him.

She jumped up and ran out the door to catch Natalia. "Natalia, look I know he's a bad guy. There was nothing going on with us. I promise I would never go back to him," Mariana pleaded.

Natalia turned around to look at Mariana and started to walk towards her, looking defeated. "Mariana, I know and we're barely even friends so either way it wouldn't matter, but this is what he always does." Natalia took her phone from her bag and handed it to Mariana. "He told me to meet him here too."

Mariana read the messages that Gabriel sent to Natalia. *Almost exactly the same as what he had sent to me.* "I'm sorry, Natalia," Mariana said, ashamed. She kept her head down out of embarrassment. For a second, she went against everything she had believed before and thought maybe he could have changed, but he hadn't.

Natalia composed herself. Mariana asked Natalia if she was okay and like always Natalia lied and said that she was.

"You don't always have to be okay. You can be honest with yourself sometimes," Mariana said, trying to get Natalia to open up. "Come on, let's go inside. We can talk it over with some coffee."

Natalia smiled and they both walked into the cafe.

As they walked back into the cafe, they were surprised to see Gabriel still there and sweating bullets.

"Oh hey." He stuttered his words. "You guys know each other?"

The girls looked at each other and laughed at him.

"Yeah, we do," Natalia replied sharply, full of attitude.

"Yeah, we met yesterday and bonded over our mutual regret: dating you," Mariana continued, and with that, they both walked away with their arms linked.

After they got their drinks and were situated, they talked. Natalia told her all about her job as an immigration lawyer and how hard she had worked to become as successful as she is now.

"That's so great Natalia," Mariana said, congratulating Natalia.

"Thank you, Mari. What do you do for work?" Natalia asked as she took a sip of her coffee.

"Oh, the question I hate the most! Um, I'm a receptionist at a *very* low-key magazine company. It gives me a lot of time to write while sitting at my desk all day. I want to be a writer, but it's hard to get started, you know. My *one-shot* was apparently given to me because Gabriel called in a favor to a friend, which is why I met him here today." Mariana tried to keep a small smile to show that even though it wasn't the best situation she was okay. "Oh, and I write a very personal blog about mental health."

Natalia's eyebrows raised at the mention of the blog. "Wow, that is really nice. What inspired you to do that?" Natalia asked curiously.

Mariana explained how she had known and seen many people struggle with mental health. "It's a topic people shy away from because it's tough to start a conversation about it. I also started my blog because of people like me," she continued to explain how she herself struggled with mental health. She described her anxiety and depression and how she dealt with it in her own time. She created the blog to make people feel less alone and create a space for people to open up about their own struggles.

"I also struggle with mental health, but I never talk about it, because like you said, I feel like it'll make me seem weak. I just choose to deal with everything alone or pour myself into my work. All I do is work," Natalia said, feeling like a weight was taken off her shoulders. It felt good to get that all out.

"Nat, no matter how you cope, your feelings are valid, and sharing them doesn't make you weak. It makes you stronger. It's not fun to always wear a mask, acting like you're happy when you're not and it's even harder to get used to taking that mask off, but it's better to have it off. Without it, you can actually breathe and be the real you," Mariana said, trying to have her friend understand being true to herself is not a bad thing.

After that day, Natalia shared her feelings with people close to her and she learned that it's okay to not be okay.

We're here for you

No matter what you're struggling with, reach out, even when it's hard. Mental health matters.

If you or someone you know needs help finding support or crisis resources, please refer them to the National Suicide Prevention Lifeline:

The National Suicide Prevention Lifeline: 1-800-273-8255

Black Blood – 5 Poems
by Naujda Davis-Van Hook, Age 12

Blues Clues

As the clouds of war fade away
I swear that it's over now,
Sun shining high in the sky, and the angels flying down
And a beautiful blissful rainbow,
As a promise not to flood my world with tears once more.

Black Blood

The black blood runs in my veins.
It runs thick and dark.
And will continue to run
For an everlasting time.
The black blood.
Let it flow.
Let it flow like lava.
Let it boil like magma.
Let it invade my body.
Let its waves pull me in.
Like the ocean reaching for the stars.
Let it crash and let it run.
Run like the speed of light.
And,
Let it have the light.
The light it never thought it would have.

Luminescence

Below the hill and under the treetops.
On this clear starry cerulean night.
Your deep red petals give off an enthralling, radiant light.
Up the hill and beyond the treetops.
The moon is high like noon, it isn't sunny but there is warmth within you. Oh the moonlight, a stunning glow is laid upon you.
Your light bouncing off the trees like mirrors in an enclosed room.
My eyes ran down from the moon, the stars, the trees, and right down to you.
Your mesmerizing beauty, I couldn't seem to pull away.
Crystalizing droplets on your green leaves as if you cried all day.
Your serrated thorns protecting you, like a fragile display.
Scars on your deep red petals that won't ever fade away.
Can I save you?
I reach to embrace you and out of the sea of stars it rains,
Suddenly I feel a twang of sadness, envy, and pain.
A big crack boom bang.
I hear a voice calling my name,
A warm but firm grasp on my wrist.
I'm snatched off my feet,
As we lock eyes and I melt away.
In a world of black and white, you are like a blank page
No color, no words, just nourishing silence.

In a world of black and white, which colored pencil should meet the sky? In this coloring book, I am confined
In this world of black and white, your color remains undefined, but you are truly a beauty to my eyes.

Welcome to Hertz Hall

The radiant sounds of the violin.
Made my heart fly as the hertz echoed through the hall.
Unleashing the colors that danced as if they had been trapped for millions of years.
The deep sound of the cello.
Emulating the bellow of the whale.
Hoping to reach my soul, as if it wanted to be loved once more.
The rich sounds of the piano.
Screaming freedom, which made my worries go away.
As if it knew every inch of my promised neverland better than me.

Valentine's Day

I asked him if he'd love me forever
He said, "What do you mean?"
I took a knife and pierced it into my chest
Carving out the token of my love
Leaving a river of blood on the floor as I…
Tore out my heart and handed it to him whole!
I ran the knife up my chest and pressed it into my face,
And carved out my dark, chocolate, candy eyes that he used to stare into
With a burning passion
Oh, the look on his face was worth it all…
"Happy Valentine's day".

The Art of a Black Girl - 5 Poems
by Clover Waddell, Age 12

Dear Covid

We're stuck in a **loop** that's dented and destroyed.

You don't even care that you're hurting us. Popping up in different places, you can't even make up your mind.
I have no idea who you are,
yet you still wanna take **innocent** lives.

I don't understand why you have so much hate. You kill for fun and in a haste, you grab us so quickly,
<u>you're unexpected.</u>
You're the invisible man but not as hectic. You kill
with stealth and without trust.
All you want to see is the world combust.

I'm really sad about what you've done.
You shouldn't be proud
that you've become the number one murderer in the entire world.

You've taken countless lives and the numbers go HIGHER as the days go by.
I don't know why
you make us quarantine, isolate, and ruin our dreams.
So many possibilities we used to have until you came along and decided to drag us all down with you because of your misery.

I **HATE** you Covid
but I hope you know we will soon be closing the curtains to your HORRIFIC show.

Survivor

I SURVIVED.

That's my goal. I want to be able to say I made it through all the hardships and sadness the world threw.

I SURVIVED.

No one understands the power of these two words. How much emotion they convey.

I SURVIVED.

Everyone goes through different problems. There›s always an antagonist in the mix. We feel so hurt, so weak, so dismissed. But, we should know that we're not alone, everyone feels somewhat unknown to this weird confusing world.

I SURVIVED.

Especially as a person of color, life twists in so many different ways. Having to conform to all these expectations, life seems to become an obligation to do what others want. I am myself and that will not change. **I stand tall, I am strong, I did nothing wrong.** I hope someday we will all understand, we are all equal!

Maybe I'm not yet ready to say I completely survived, but I am ready to say I will always continue to *thrive*.

The Art of a Black Girl

Damaged self-esteem
Trying to be a *QUEEN*
Why are we never heard, but we're seen?

Being black is a struggle especially as a girl. Everyone's telling us what to do, saying this game is fair.
This game is not fair! Do you even know my name, or am I just the black girl trespassing through your domain? I pray every day that things will finally change.

The real question I should ask is why do you bring us down? Why do you take time to break all our sound? It honestly doesn't make sense to me, but we'll continue to RiSe, just you wait and see.

Look! We're starting to come up, our vision is clear, all of us black girls are nearly in tears. Tears of joy, glee, triumph, and delight!

All of us black girls unite for change, justice, and respect. I fight for me, I fight for you, I fight to change everyone's mindset.

Triple Threat

I don't think you seem to realize how hidden I am, I don't show my true self, It's hard to see that I have to alter myself to fit in, to be with the crowd and have many friends.

But, what I've begun to realize It's just me, myself, and I, and that's all I need to fly.

Fly over the hatred, judging, and fear.

Fly over the people that harass what I wear, how I talk, how I act.

Is everything here just about a pact to become who you want me to be? To become the person who's begging on their knees apologizing for something I didn't do.

You do realize you want me to hide more, you want me in a mask, and behind a closed door.

No!

I won't get sucked into all these lies. I will allow myself to *soar and fly*, like an eagle that lives life carefree.

<u>My freedom is something you will not take from me.</u>

I'm strong and empowered, I'm a dang triple threat! **Brains, Bravery, and Beauty.**

You don't scare me, you and your little pets.

I understand that some of you are under their control,

but hopefully, you can find some petrol to fuel your potential, all that greatness that you have.

It's there, but you want to stay in the pact. Don't stay in the group c'mon let's fly and be free. We can escape and live happily.

Me and you don't have to be stuck in these chains.

I am myself and that will NEVER change.

~Tired~

Growing up is a hard thing
There are too many expectations
There's never enough room to *breathe*
Don't you get it, We can't *breathe!*

There's no room to speak
We can't have an opinion because we're too young to know anything
We're too young to be included in **those** conversations
Our jobs are to listen, comprehend, and ask NO questions

We're also not seen
Everyone expects us to just smile and be happy
They're so surprised when we seem fed up and done.

Because at this point, we're **extremely** tired
Tired of not being heard
Tired of not being seen
Tired of being told that we don't have enough experience to have **those** conversations

We know more about the world than we should at our age because everything is poisoned
Our minds
Our bodies
Our hearts

Everything is falling apart. We experience so much. Too much. Yet you have the audacity to say we don't know what we're talking about

In order for us to reach our full potential, we need to participate in **those** conversations that so greatly impact our lives

Each and everyone one of us are ready to be heard, seen, and included.

The real question is are you ready for us?

Cat Tale: The Prophecy of a Dream

by Alanna Williams, Age 15

I awoke, straining to see. I found myself drenched in ice water, cold and shivering on the ground. I had somehow managed to teleport to this place while I was sleeping. Was that even possible? My bones ached. And inside of my head there was a merciless pounding, activated by each of my thoughts. It was cold. A feeling of cold I had never felt before. As I fully opened my eyes, a heavy, dark fog surrounded me. Where was I? Why is no one else around? I took a breath in, and it felt as if my lungs were being filled with icy crystals. And when I took a breath out, a putrefied smokey mist escaped from my almost frozen lips. I coughed and wheezed. The temperature dropped by the minute. I attempted to flip onto my chest and then get up, but my balance shifted dramatically. Goosebumps shot down my arms, making my hair stand straight up. My legs were like lead and my vision blurred. Right at that moment a shrill burst of cold wind flew past me. It was as if it were made up of pure darkness. I yelled out. But, of course, there was no response.

"Help!" I screamed. I fell to the ground. Too weak to go on.

"Ms. Williams! There is no sleeping in class! Do not make me have to write you up," an irritated Mr. Markinson said.

I sat right up, shaking a bit.

"I am so sorry, Sir, it—it won't happen again," I said. Jeez, I couldn't believe I dozed off in class. But that meant all of it was just a dream. Which was weird because it felt so real...

"Hey, Layla is everything okay? You never fall asleep in class," my best friend Amber said as we made our way down the school hallway.

We walked out to the court in front of school. I paused and thought about what I should tell her, how to respond.

"Thanks. I'm okay. Just didn't get a ton of sleep last night," I said.

"Aw yeah, I feel you. But glad to hear that you're okay. See you!"

I walked off to my next class, my brain a mess. As the day went by, I struggled through a daze-like feeling of chilled discomfort. When school was finally over, I grabbed my stuff and headed home. Little did I know that soon everything would change. My life and really myself. And so I walked home that day, not knowing that ice water had been dripping from my clothes.

It is a stormy night. Just a few days after the first strange dream had occurred, I lie awake from the sound of terrifying thunder and a mysterious howling of the wind. A chill creeps up my spine. I wrap my blanket tighter around me. Ever since that day at school I have trouble falling asleep. I'm not sure why, but I keep getting this feeling. It's almost impossible to explain—but it is here.

Very much here.

It lingers around me like a shadow. Follows me, almost watching me. Like a predator stalks its prey. I check the time. It is 4:00 am.

"Ugh why can't I just fall asleep?" I whisper. I lie in bed and hope that sleep will come. I try to analyze the dream but really can't figure it out. Where was that place and why was I alone there? Was it even a dream? No, it had to be real. That dark burst of wind had been far too real.

It is a long time before my eyes finally flutter shut, but eventually they do. When I wake up, I'm met by my mother's kind smile.

"Good morning sweetie," she says. Her voice is like honey running down a muffin.

"Morning mom," I say through a yawn.

"How'd you sleep, Lay?"

"Oh, I slept all right." I reply.

She looks at me with that face. The judgmental, analytic kind that can see right through your soul.

"What?" I ask.

"Liar," she answers.

I laugh. My mom is psychic after all, and not just one of those kooky ones you see on the boardwalk but a real one. She practices all these different chakra balancing techniques, tarot card reading, and does psychic evaluations. I love my mom. She is basically my hero.

"What's going on, hun? I feel that something's off with you. A sort of imbalance."

"I'm okay, I just didn't get a ton of sleep and have a lot on my mind," I say.

"Ok, well, let me know if you wanna talk about it more," she says, and she walks out of my room.

I get ready for school. I grab breakfast, say goodbye to my mom and just as I am ready to head out the door, my dad stops me.

"You headed to school, Lay lay?" he asks in his usual funky tone.

"Yes, dad." I roll my eyes a little.

"All right, just make sure you have something to eat. See you after school." He gives me a big squeeze.

My dad is full of light, laughter, and corny dad jokes, but I love him dearly. As I leave, I say good morning to my neighbors, Mr. and Mrs. Harold. They have never really liked my family because we look different, but I try to stay positive and kind in the face of it all. I walk by them and receive a half smile from Mr. Harold and a nod from Mrs. Harold. When I'm past them, I can hear their whispered insults. Our neighborhood is full of people like this, privileged white couples who pretend to be open minded people but aren't. They claim they're not racist but use racial slurs when they think no one's listening. They "joke" about having black staff and think calling the police on people of color for simply being in "their" neighborhood is justifiable. It's tiring being one of the few black families in my town and the only black girl in my neighborhood. I just wish I saw more people like me. Sometimes I even wish I wasn't different. I wish I could walk down the street and have no one notice that I was there.

I make my way just a few blocks from my house and then, as I turn a corner, the ground beneath me begins to shake. An earthquake? No, it can't be. My heart starts to pound. The pavement shifts and twists below my feet and a sort of rumbling sound can be heard from all around me. It's as if the sound is closing itself in on me. I cover my ears against the deafening sound when a giant hole opens beneath me. I scream and run, try to get as far away as possible from it but I slip and fall. The hole is even bigger now, and I'm being pulled into it! I claw my way out, but the force from the hole is too strong. It sucks me in and closes up above me.

In situations like these you would think that falling down a hole would feel like an endless cycle. That you would be falling down, down, down, forever. But that's not quite how it is for me. I fall for what seems just a couple of seconds and then I come to the ground softly. It's like I floated just above and then landed. I have no idea how I had done this, but there were bigger problems to face. I have no clue as to where I am. Or if someone can even find me here.

I begin to walk.

At the end of what seems to be a long tunnel is a light. I pick up some speed and make my way closer to the illuminating light. I feel my heart pound, but I'm determined to find out what the light is and where it will lead me to.

At the end, I enter a cavern of some sort. The giant light has vanished and all around me purple crystals are lit up. It's a magnificent place and I stand in awe at it all. I can smell the scent of lilacs and honeysuckle and the ground is a sort of pillowy dirt. Magnificent vines cover the cavern's walls and I notice several interesting rocks and stones at my feet. It's all so calm and beautiful.

What is this place? And then at that moment the ground once again begins to shake. Uh Oh! Here we go. The purple crystals' light begins to flicker, and I sense that something is coming. A presence like my own? The cave begins to shimmer and sparkle. What's going on?! I'm still in shock of all that's happening, when a voice echoes through the cave. It's strong and loud and it seems as though it comes from everywhere and nowhere at the same time.

"Layla" the voice booms.

I'm surprised to hear my own name and anxiously await what else the voice has to say.

"Layla Williams?" says the voice.

It sends goosebumps down my arms.

"I have been waiting for someone like you. I have been hoping that another special being would discover this cave and find their destiny," the voice says.

"You've been waiting for someone like me? But I'm nothing special."

"On the contrary. You have something in you, Layla, and all you need is to have it unlocked. Only beings full of rich power find this place. This is meant to be," the voice once again booms.

I cannot believe what I'm hearing. Me, a special being? I refuse to believe it.

"Layla, the more you refuse to accept your destiny the worse off you will be," the voice replies.

Can it read my thoughts? "What do I need to do? How can I accept this—or my destiny?" I ask the voice.

"I cannot reveal to you everything, dear Layla. You must discover that on your own," the voice says.

"Please, you must help me. I'm lost on my own," I exclaim.

"Just believe in yourself, like I do. The changes will come. If you truly need me just summon your strength." The voice fades away. "For if what I believe is true, then you are indeed an Earthlin Fae."

"A what!?" I ask, but all is now quiet. No sounds, no anything.

The light begins to return steadily to the crystals. I stand still, in shock, and extremely confused. What did any of this mean for me? What in the world is an Earthlin whatever? I close my eyes and let out a sigh. And when I open my eyes, I'm back on the street.

I look around, blinking wildly.

No hole.

Was this some sort of daydream? I could've sworn this time that it was all real.

"Oh well." I head off to school with a strange lightness in my step.

The day goes by fast. I stay focused on my work and am surprised that I'm able to because in the back of my mind I am thinking and thinking about the world I visited underground. Had that magical place really been real? Or was it just something from my imagination? The voice had seemed pretty real, and if it was, that meant that something was going to happen to me. The voice said I was "a special being" and that I needed to figure out what changes were to come. Ugh. It all seemed like nonsense. Maybe I should tell someone. But what would they think? The story is pretty unbelievable.

On my way home, a searing pain starts in my gums. It's sharp, almost like animal teeth are forming. It can't be. I keep going over what I should do as I continue walking, when a hand reaches out and touches my shoulder. I turn suddenly and hiss!

It's Amber.

"Jeez Layla, what was that??" she asks. She trembles in her surprise.

"I don't know..." I say slowly. I look down to see my hands almost morphing between human ones and animal paws. I blink several times. Does Amber see this too?

"Hey, I gotta go." The words fumble out before I quickly walk away. I feel worried and really just need someone, anyone to talk to. But how can I explain this? Once I'm home, I find my parents getting dinner ready. I should tell them. But when I begin to make my way over to them my mom stumbles and then collapses.

"Mom, are you okay!?" I ask, completely startled at what had just happened.

My dad and I help her regain her balance and she makes it over to a chair.

"Yes, I'm fine sweetie, just had an alarming amount of spiritual energy come my way," she says clearly, a bit surprised herself.

"Are you sure you're all right?" my dad asks.

"Yes, I'm sure. It's just that I could have sworn it was…well, never mind," she exclaims looking at us both with a sense of wonder in her eyes.

My dad is puzzled. He shrugs, scratches his head, and walks off to finish dinner.

"Mom don't worry, it was probably just some sort of false alarm," I try to reassure her.

"Well, that's just it, Layla. It wasn't random. I felt a strong wave of it come right from you," she says with worry and a sort of disbelief.

I am completely taken aback. Mystical Spirit energy coming from me!? What did that even mean?

After dinner I go off to bed, but my mind is spinning fast, like one of those rides at the fair. If that cavern place had been real, then the two things must be connected. Maybe this was part of the changes the voice said would come. I toss and turn all night, my head a volcano of thoughts. When morning finally comes, I have made up my mind. "I'm going to tell someone," I say firmly, springing up from my bed. I start to get ready but, all of a sudden, I feel terribly sick. I run to the bathroom and much to my surprise cough up a—hairball? I leap back, then laugh. No way! I rinse the wad of slimy white-ish grey hair down the sink.

The next day I rush to school and search and search for my best friend Amber. I finally come across her walking through the front gate and am so relieved to have found her.

"Amber, I have very important information!" I half yell at her.

"Whoa Layla, slow down," Amber exclaims, clearly surprised by my huffing and puffing.

"I really need to talk to you," I say.

"Can it wait until after class because we don't wanna be late." She begins to walk off.

"No Amber, it really can't wait," I exclaim. I can tell she just wants to go to class. I pause, hold my breath. "I think I'm an Earthlin something or other," I whisper.

"What's going on Layla?" Amber asks. "You've been acting so strange lately and..."

"I know," I cut her off. "And I'm going to explain everything." So, I do. I tell her about what has been going on that day and really for weeks. I even explain how I have been so confused with all that was going on and that it was the reason I had been acting so weird. Once I finish telling her everything, she doesn't laugh or walk away. Instead, she gives me a hug. I hug her back. I'm so glad to have gotten it all off my chest.

"So why didn't you tell me any of this before?" she asks.

"I'm not sure. I mean I wanted to, but it all sounds so crazy, and I thought you wouldn't believe me." I looked away a little ashamed.

"I do. But I also think you need to stop worrying so much," she says.

"I never said I was worried," I grumble.

"That's just it. You didn't have to. I can just tell," Amber says. She holds back a laugh.

"Whatever." I roll my eyes trying not to smile. "I just don't want anything else bad or weird to happen," I say, as we make our way towards the front of school and hurry to class.

"That's understandable. So, let's both hope for no more surprises," she agrees.

"Hey Layla, remember the other day when I startled you?" Amber asks, as we sit for lunch.

A strange feeling starts to rise inside of me. "Uh no, why?" I lie.

"Well, it's hard to explain but..." she scoots closer to me and lowers her voice. "It was like you changed. I don't know how, but you became something else."

"That's crazy, Amber!" I attempt to ignore the ever growing feeling that is only getting stronger. "What might I have turned into?" I nervously wait for her response.

"A cat" Amber says, her face serious but her tone relaxed. Like she's testing me?

I spring up from the lunch table and hurry to the bathroom. Amber silently follows after me. I switch on the light and am amazed to see myself with a tail! I jump and then feel the long, furry, tail that is now poking out of my pants, attached to my body. I pace back and forth in the bathroom completely scared out of my mind. What is happening to me?

A familiar voice reaches me. "Layla. Layla. Where did you go?!" a hushed Amber calls out.

I panic. I can't let her find me. I decide to sneak out of school because I don't want anyone to see me with a tail. Especially not

Amber. Without hesitation, I creep out of the bathroom and in a dash head home. I am beyond relieved when I finally make it to my house and slowly, as quietly as I can, go up to my room. I flop onto my bed exhausted from running, but then I feel something prickly on my face. I go to feel and yell out in surprise. Whiskers have grown! I'm totally freaked out. I check in the mirror and two ears have appeared on top of my head. What am I becoming? Before I know it, I'm hyperventilating, and feel completely out of control. I end up falling and knocking myself out.

When I awake, a sense of confusion comes over me. My eyes slowly open and I look around. Everything seems the same. Except my room is several sizes bigger and it is filled with so many different smells. Weird—What happened? "Mom?" I call out, but there is no response. Strange, she always answers. A feeling of despair comes over me. My head hurts really bad. I glance over at my mirror and am shocked to see that my normal reflection is no more. Instead, a cloud-colored cat looks back at me! I have a small coffee brown colored nose and yellow beady eyes.

I jump down from my bed, my heart and mind racing. Hastily, without really thinking, I run. I can't believe what's happening. Once I make it to the street, I can feel the cool breeze through what now is my fur. It's actually quite nice. I begin to calm down as I walk around a bit and no one really notices me. I don't get looks like I did when I was a girl. I feel—free. Maybe this won't be so bad? I prance about. I guess I could get used to being a cat.

But how will I turn back?!

The words of the voice ring through my ears. "Just believe."
And so I do. At that moment I am a girl again.

Weeks go by and I get more and more comfortable switching between being a cat and being a girl. But I mostly love every second of being a cat. I have no worries and while every now and then people try to pet me, I pay no mind. I go on adventures around the town and feel like a whole new me. And the best part is when and if I want, I can turn back into a girl. Weeks turn into months and still no one has caught on. I realize how dangerous it would be if my secret were revealed. I decide not to tell Amber or my parents yet for fear that they will tell others about my power. There's no telling how my parents might react and what they might do with the information. I must keep quiet, no matter what. Plus, I want it to be my secret—at least for now.

One day as I'm walking about as a girl, without paying attention I bump into two people. A huge wave of dark energy comes over me and practically paralyzes me to my core. It feels a lot like the burst of cold wind I felt a while back.

"Oh my goodness, s—so sorry," I say, quite startled. I slowly start to walk away, but then something inside me tells me to go back. "Excuse me, but do I know you?" I begin to turn around. But when I look, I see that the people are gone. I continue to walk, puzzled as to how they disappeared from my sight.

Then I hear Amber's voice "Layla! Thank god I found you." She pulls up beside me and rolls down the window of her silver Fiat.

"Hey Amber—what's up?" I ask, a little alarmed to see her.

"Just get in, I'll explain everything on the way," she says.

It's suddenly hours later. The roads are long and seem to only get longer. I watch the headlights of the cars in front of us blink all together, almost in sync. Putrid cold air blasts through from the AC vents. I'm uncomfortable, not just from the chill inside the car, but also from the haziness outside.

"This should be working by now. I rewired this thing to act as a location finder, a sort of RD8 device if you will, but the signal still seems weak," Amber explains, her brows furrowed in frustration.

I look at her blankly as I'm not too familiar with technological stuff.

Seeing my puzzled expression, she goes on. "Oh, just think of it as a high-level GPS tracking system. Like...from the *Incredibles*!" she beams.

"Yeah, I don't think I want to be thinking or talking about a movie right now," I respond, quite snappy.

"Right—sorry, my bad," she croaks.

"Amber, where the heck are you taking me and why did it have to be now!"

She pauses and looks at me with her big moon-like eyes. "There's somewhere important we need to go," she says. She turns away as she abruptly swerves the car in a U-turn.

We eventually make it to a huge building. On the side in bold letters, it says Laboratory of Independent Studies.

"Why are we here?" I ask Amber, quite confused.

"I followed you home when you tried to sneak away and saw you transforming. I wasn't totally sure, but I waited for you outside and when the door to your house opened a cat came out. All those times you weren't yourself. Added to the fact that you wouldn't really talk about it. Also, I know for a fact you don't have a cat" she explains, her mouth coming into a smile. I was taken aback.

"You know…" I sighed.

"Of course, I know. I'm your best friend and why else would we be here!" she responds through a laugh.

"So, *what* is this place? And how did you find it?" I ask, as Amber takes me to a back door.

"After I saw you fully turn. I began researching. Everything has to do with the fantastical. I found out about this place and what kind of research they did here. It all had to do with Faes, other mythical creatures, and strange powers. So, I drove here hoping to get more information, but they're closed," she admits.

"Okay—so we can come back tomorrow?" I urge, still confused.

"Layla, they're closed for good," Amber exclaims. She kicks in the door.

"Whoa, so we're just breaking in?" I gasp.

"Not really. It's abandoned, plus it's for a good cause!"

As we make our way inside, I whip out my phone's flashlight and begin to look around.

"Layla, over here," Amber calls out.

I follow her voice and end up at a huge library. Thousands of books sit on shelves and piles of paper, records, and other files lay scattered among the library tables. I marvel at all that is around me. This library is probably the biggest one I have ever seen.

"If you wanna learn more about what you are, this is the place to do it" Amber says brightly.

"Can't you just tell me what you know?" I ask.

"I could—but it would be better if you read everything for yourself," Amber explains.

So, I gather as many books as I can and begin to read.

Several hours pass, until I finally come across a section on different Faes and their history. "Wait, now I remember. The voice had said that I was an Earthlin Fae. I just didn't know what that meant," I say, excitedly. "It says here that Earthlin Faes are a type of mystical being that are known to be very powerful. They come from the planet Maerta which is a place very similar to Earth. It's all right here!" I say with glee. "Earthlins are wonderful shape-shifters and usually blend right in. Many strange sightings have occurred, and it is now thought that these creatures roam the Earth," I read. "Can you believe that!" I shout over to Amber as she looks up from reading a huge book of magical history.

"You might want to read this part too," she says, solemnly handing me the book.

I begin to read and my newfound excitement slowly withers to dust. The book tells of a terribly devastating war that had gone on between Earthlin Faes and some other beings called Etherians. The planet of Maerta ended up being destroyed with nothing of it remaining. "I—I don't understand, how could this happen?" My voice breaks.

"It wasn't easy to find, but I dug for it. Etherians were known to be very loving, loyal, and beautiful beings," Amber says. "They protected and looked out for everyone and had a magnificent planet. The people of Maerta were jealous, and sought out the Etherians in a cold-blooded war, one the Etherians didn't want to fight. It ended with many of the Etherian people dead and their lands destroyed. This ruined the peace that the Etherian people had tried to keep and turned them all to be consumed with evil and hatred."

I can barely comprehend what I've heard.

"That's not all. It also says that out of vengeance the Etherians attempted to hunt down every last Earthlin Fae."

"So, all of them are just gone?" I ask in disbelief.

"I think so, except you..." she replies, in a hushed manner.

I drop down to the floor on my knees. The shock hits me hard. "I'm the last one."

That's when a huge crash comes from outside.

"What was that!?" Amber yelped. She grabs the biggest book before we run outside to the front of the building. Much to our surprise we are met by two very strange looking beings. Both float mid-air, right above what was Amber's car and now is a wrecked pile.

"If it isn't the last little Earthlin herself," one of the beings snickers.

"Finally come out to play?" the other jabs.

"Who are you and what do you want?" I question aggressively.

Amber flips violently through the pages of the book. She grabs my arm. "Layla, look at the markings on their hands. Those are sacred symbols from Etheria. They're Etherians!" she warns.

"Ahh you humans are clever aren't you?" the being who seems to be female exclaims.

"I don't know, Natalia—but something good!" the male being shrieks.

I get a better look at their faces. They're the same people I ran into earlier!

"Whatever you want you won't get it here" Amber yells.

In a flash the beings throw several bursts of energy toward her before laughing wildly.

She's pushed back by the force.

"Oh god, Amber!" I scream in fright. I run back to her.

"Don't worry about me. Just focus on beating them, I'm okay." Amber's voice is stifled by the pain.

"I—I don't think I can. There's no way I'd win."

"You can, Layla. I believe in you. Just use the power within!"

The same cold and empty energy I felt from the beings before comes over me. What does that mean? I'm sorry, Amber, but I can't do it. My powers aren't strong enough. Fear creeps up into me. The sentence replays over and over in my head, until I am covered by self-doubt, judgement, and disbelief. The beings circle around Amber and I and shoot another blast of energy. I jump out of the way but not in enough time to completely protect my arm. I close my eyes, then open them to find myself back in the horribly cold, desolate, dark place from what I thought was just a dream.

"It's real! It's all real," I stutter. I shiver like crazy. I hold my bleeding arm tightly, pain surging through it as I trudge along, each step becoming heavier than the next. I focus and wish as hard as I can, but I'm still stuck. My eyes start to practically freeze shut.

But then the kind voice's words strike me. Almost like I hear them for the first time.

"Just *believe*..."

I had always thought that the voice meant 'believe in your new powers' but what it really meant was 'believe in yourself.' It is something so simple, yet I never fully acknowledged it before. All of the things I tried to erase or ignore about myself were what made me a powerful being. It's why I found the voice and my destiny.

My mind flashes back to what Amber said, "Use the power within."

"Of course!" I shout. My differences which I have lived with all my life are more powerful than the shape-shifting abilities I'd harnessed just a couple months ago. I am no longer afraid. I know I can do this.

My eyes shot open.

I was ready to fight.

The clash of Past and Present
by Chariot Waddell, Age 14

My name is Sandra Johns and I do not want to be here right now. I really don't want to spend a beautiful Friday afternoon listening to a white woman talk about the civil rights movement, but here I am. In my opinion, they could've just hired a Black person educated on my history to do this tour. But there are little to no Black people in Bisbee, Arizona so it makes sense why Ms. Powell is giving it. The manager said she has a degree in "African American History" so she qualifies... In a daze, I perfunctorily trace the picture of a lion engraved into the shiny golden locket that hangs around my neck. My sister Barbara gave it to me for my sixteenth birthday this year and the gold on it is so shiny most of the time it seems to glow... But when she attempts to educate us about how **Rosa Parks was the first Black woman to exercise civil disobedience on a Montgomery bus**, I snap out of the daze and my hand immediately shoots up.

"That's not true Ms. Powell. Actually, a fifteen-year-old girl named Claudette Colvin was the first to exercise civil disobedience on a Montgomery bus."

All my peers turn towards me, their eyes filled with disapproval because I thought to correct her!? Our area of the museum is silent.

I tap my foot on the floor waiting for the silence to dilute.

Finally, Mrs. Powell speaks. "Well, that's the information I was told." And with a turn on her heel, she sashays away, leading the rest of my class to the next exhibit.

I usually don't get angry at misinformed white women because I'm a Black girl... Need I say more? But for some reason, today, I am angry, and my blood begins to boil at the fact that it is 2020 and white Americans are still not properly educated on the Civil Rights Movement. Still. Even though it is a large part of our country's past and to this very day exists in the form of the Black Lives Matter Movement.

To let off some steam I turn to my sister Barbara and whisper, "Remember when we were younger, we would play that Black History Matching Game where you would have to match a card filled with a snippet of information about who that person was and then the other card was a picture of that person?"

"I do remember that! We would spend hours at the table playing that game. Your eyes would always light up and you would shriek so loudly when you had the most matches. It was hilarious!" Barbara chuckles.

"That's the game this lady needs to play."

A loud laugh escapes Barbara's mouth and she clears her throat just in time for Mrs. Powell to give her the side eye. "Agreed."

"Lunch break kids!" Mrs. Powell exclaims.

As most of my classmates scramble towards the museum's stale-smelling gift store filled with keychains and magnets,

I decide I want off to "explore" the museum (and fact check information about my history) by myself. Right as I take a step away from the glass doors of course, I hear someone call my name.

"Sandra..." Barbara scream whispers, "Where are you going?"

"I'm going to check out the museum. Duh."

"Can I come?"

"No. If both of us are gone, two of the only Black kids in the class, she'll get suspicious."

"Whateva. Just hurry up, ok? I don't want you to get in trouble."

"In trouble for what, Barb? I'm exploring the museum. Oh my gosh, you're such a goody two shoes."

"Yeah, I know," she says with a smirk.

I love Barbara and I want her to come with me on my "adventure." Although we are only nine months apart, I'm still the older sister. I wouldn't want both of us to get in trouble.

After checking if the coast is clear (again) I walk away from the glass doors and into the core of the museum. To the left of me is a tiny room with a few pieces of African art and sculptures. As I walk farther down the hallway Chuck Berry's song, Johnny B. Good, drifts into my ear and touches my soul. I look over to see a vinyl record spinning on a Victrola, amplifying the beautiful melody and a picture of his guitar "Maybellene" placed above it, on a bright red wall. My daddy played this song after school one day just two weeks before the 5th grade talent show and Barbara and I immediately wanted to perform it. He attempted to teach me the keys on my baby blue electric guitar, Gus, and my mom was coaching Barbara on how to sing it like the King of Rock himself. That performance was a masterpiece... to Barbara and me. Our parents knew it was a train wreck, but in the pictures you see 5th grade versions of us smiling with ruby red roses in our arms, our eyes filled with pride. I don't understand how Barb possessed that much confidence to go up on stage and sing in front of over 200 kids at the time. Now public speaking is like her number one fear.

When I finally find it in me to depart from my new favorite exhibit something catches my eye. Placed against the left corner of the museum, I spy a statue of an African American teenage girl made from copper. The copper statue shines against the white walls in the dim light of the museum, She holds her hand out almost as if to say stop, to warn the museum goers about something dangerous that lurks ahead. There is a small gold plate at the foot of the statue that is engraved with the words, "It seemed like reaching for the moon." To the side of the statue stands a podium that reads: Her name was Barbara Rose Johns, and she was sixteen years old. She was a civil rights activist.

I can't, I just can't. Kinda creepy how she has the same exact name as my sister, but I'm also amused by how vague the description is. I just start talking to the statue right then and there.

"Girl... I just can't with white people sometimes. How are they gonna put you on display like this and not give an adequate description of what you accomplished. You were a sixteen-year-old making change in the world." I just chuckle. I pull my phone out of my pocket. "Hey Google, who was Barbara Rose Johns?"

"Here are results for who pulled the biggest rose con."

"No, who was Barbara Rose Johns?" I say, overenunciating every word.

Google reads a snippet from the first article that pops up. "Barbara Rose Johns was one of the first teenagers to lead her whole student body in a protest to advocate against the horrific learning conditions of their school." she explains in her monotone, robotic voice.

I click on the article and learn Barbara attended Robert Russa Moton High School in Farmville, Prince Edward County, Virginia. They had to learn out of coal tar shacks and received textbooks from the surrounding all-white schools with derogatory words written in bold letters across the pages. Because Moton High was an all-Black school the white administration didn't want to provide them with funds or resources to thrive and Barbara was tired of it.

As I examine the statue, I notice that Barbara is wearing the same lion engraved gold locket that my sister and I wear. Just to make sure, I remove the locket from my neck and place it directly next to hers just to make sure.

Zaaaaaaap!

"Owwwwww," I say as my locket falls to the floor. Did my locket just zap me or was that my imagination? I pick it up and I examine it. Was it all in my head? But as I hold the locket, I begin to feel really dizzy. So, I stumble to the nearest bench and sit down. I close my eyes to try to stop the room from spinning. Breathe, I tell myself. 1...2...3.

Suddenly overwhelmed with a tingling sensation I open my eyes and... oh my gosh I can feel my throat closing and it becomes hard to breathe. I close my eyes again and whisper to myself, "This is not the museum." My face starts to feel swollen and my body feels numb. The smell of sweat and corn chips wafts into my nose. When I try to open my eyes my vision blurs. The world is spiraling to me. It's about to collapse. I'm about to throw up... Get it together Sandra this is just a dream! You're actually safe at the museum about to go back to your class. It takes me three minutes to compose myself. When I open my eyes, I realize that this is not a dream... This is reality.

I sit on a similar bench in a place full of Black people my age. The statues are not there which is the first clue to knowing I'm not in Bisbee, Arizona anymore. I no longer see the copper statue but instead, I see girls dressed in dresses that are cinched at the hip, the material flowing outwards from the waist while the guys are wearing pleated pants and sweater vests. The stucco wall is cracked and water drips on the floor. A basketball net hangs above the bench and the painted words across the gymnasium/auditorium wall read "Motown High."

What the heck?!!

Wait, wasn't Motown High where Barbara Rose Johns went?!?! How did I get here? I reach for my phone out of my jeans pocket to call for help but then I realize I don't have pockets and I have no phone?!?! I have so many questions!

The whole room is filled with hustle and bustle and accompanied by teenage chaos. I hear pieces of conversation everywhere around me.

On one side of the room, I hear, "That music is jammin! Hey Shorty, turn that up!"

On another side a girl says, "Okay, so this is the route we would make in order to circle around back to the school."

"So, two weeks is how long you expect school to be postponed in order to get the message across?" one guy says to another.

In this orchestra of voices, I hear my name come from the stage. A girl who looks familiar stands at a wood podium that has had the names of students scratched into it a million times over. The girl taps a pencil on her lips.

The voice says, "Sandra, come here sis. I need to run something by you."

As I approach this girl, multiple questions race through my mind. Questions like: Who is this girl claiming to be my sister? What should I do? Should I ask her questions about why I am in a gymnasium? She seems like she will be able to answer them. Okay, now we're talking, that's a good idea. Now, what should I say? What's up, sister! No, no, that's not right. How about...hey girl, hey! No, no that's not it.

As I walk up the stage stairs and approach my "sister" I spot a date written in the top right corner of her paper and I freeze. My eyes widen and my heartbeat reverberates throughout my body as

I whisper to myself the date on her paper. "April 15, 1951," I repeat it. "April 15, 1951."

"Hey, sis... what's up," I say hesitantly, the words stumbling out my mouth.

Now the only question that is nestled on the tip of my tongue is... Why am I in 1951? I have watched enough time travel movies to know that I simply cannot ask Barbara anything about this matter or tell her I'm from 2020. If I do, it will rip a hole in the space-time continuum, and everything will down spiral!

"Earth to Sandra! It's your sister Barbara speaking from planet earth!"

I went into a daze again. I snap out of it as soon as I digest what she just said.

"Barbara," I say. "Um sorry, Barb, what were you saying?" I pretend everything is fine, but I'm astounded that this girl who claims she is my sister actually has my sister's name. Everything about her screams my sister. She looks similar to my sister but dressed in different clothing and different style of makeup. She has the same demeanor and aura as my sister. The only difference between her and my sister is that they exist in different time periods!

"I was saying how I need some ideas for the speech I have to say to the student body on Monday."

"Ummm... well, what point are you trying to get across?"

"Sandra, you know what point I'm trying to get across. I'm trying to convince the whole student body to protest the conditions of *our* school!"

"Well, why can't you just say it from the heart? Why does it need to be planned?"

"Because this will probably be one of the most important speeches I'll ever give, and if I want it to be perfect, I know it needs to be planned and memorized."

"Oh, okay," I say aloud, but in my mind, I'm thinking: Planning!? Now I know for sure that this is my sister. I have a headache now and just want to lie down at this point! I really wish this was a dream, but I'm not sure it is with how vivid and surreal everything seems.

My sister begins to speak to the entire audience. "Okay, guys, after months of planning we finally have everything ironed out!"

A chorus of cheers erupts from all sides of the room.

"Make sure to be on time on Monday bright and early so our protest can run smoothly and effectively. See you all Monday!" Barbara says. "Come on Sandra, let's go."

As we walk to the bus stop my mouth just hangs wide open. There are shops with large, colorful signs on the front. They read "eggs for 19 cents" or "this is the best candy shop in town, folks."

There are classy, exotic cars parked on curbs in hues of red, turquoise, and yellow. Little girls in saddleback shoes jumping rope, their rhythmic songs with catchy tunes ringing in my ears. I see guys (super cute guys) my age at the baseball field screaming and shouting at one another as a white and red ball swirls through the air. Out of habit, I wave to them to say hi, but when Barbara smacks my hand down the reality really settles in that this *is* 1951.

"Sandy, you know it's against the rules to wave to a bunch of white boys! What has gotten into you lately! Is everything okay?"

"No, everything is not okay. Apparently, I'm in 1951, you're my sister. I have no idea how to get home, and..." I pause mid-sentence when I see the confused and worried look on Barbara's face.

She places the back of her hand on my forehead. "Sandy, if you don't have a fever why are you acting like this? You, my big sister, have been acting weird ever since our meeting today. Are you scared about the protest?"

"Yes," I lie, not knowing what else to tell her. Although the truth is I'm stuck in 1951 not knowing how I got here and no way to get out.

"Sandy, it's going to be okay. I'm scared too, but you don't see me going around acting like I don't know where I am and that I'm not old enough to know not to wave to a bunch of white boys even if they are fine."

"Sandra!?!?!" I chuckle.

She starts laughing so I start laughing knowing in my heart everything is going to be okay.

As I lay in bed that night cloaked by moonlight, I recall what I know so far. Apparently, I am in Prince Edward County, Virginia, in April 1951. My sister is the "Barbara Rose Johns" and on Monday we will lead a protest to fight the substandard conditions at Robert Russa Moton High School. I am her sister Sandra who traveled here from 2020, Bisbee, Arizona. But the real question is, how did I get here?!

Wait... wait one minute... I just had an epiphany!!!! It was the lockets!!!! The statue of Barbara in the museum was wearing the same locket as me and they must have a connection with each other and for some crazy reason, it brought me here!!!! While I seriously am excited to take part in the protest, previously only experiencing them in history books, I have to figure out a way to get home.

"Hey Barbara, you up?"

"Yes."

"Do you have a locket that hangs around your neck?"

"Yes."

"Who gave it to you?"

"Mommy gave both of us the lockets when we were babies, remember? Our lockets both have lions engraved into them."

I jump up and take off my locket, coming around her bed to place my locket next to hers.

When I place it next to hers, we both witness a small spark between the lockets, but it doesn't bring me back to the museum.

Barbara's mouth drops to the floor when she sees the spark. "Sandy, did you see th-tha-that spark between our lockets?"

"What spark?" I say knowing damn well what's she talking about, but not wanting to alarm her.

"THE SPARK, the strip of blue light I just saw travel from the locket around my neck to yours!" she whispers screams, her hot breath hitting my face.

"Barbara, maybe you need some rest," I say, resting my head on her forehead.

"Maybe I do." Within a matter of seconds, she drifts off into a deep sleep.

"Sandy, wake up, it's time to go to school!"

"Uhhhhhhhhh, leave me alone."

"Meet you downstairs, we leave in twenty minutes."

As Barbara runs downstairs already prepared for the day, I have no idea where to start. I am not in my normal environment! I don't have a toothbrush or my normal hair products. I don't even know where the soap is! I attempt to fall in line with my "family" or as they say it in this era "get into the swing of things."

When Barbara and I walk to the bus awaiting ahead of us, I try to take in my surroundings but this time with a new perspective. I see signs all around us that say, "Colored Only" and "White Only". It's crazy how there is division around every corner just because of people's skin color.

But it's not like that has changed in 2020.

We walk up the stairs of the bus, greet the white bus driver, and get settled into seats in the row right behind the white section. Barbara and I are in the same row but don't share the same seats but instead, we are sitting on the seats closest to the walkway. While I sit next to a large Black woman reading a book on coding, she sits next to a Black man dressed in a suit and glasses gazing off into the distance.

Right as Barbara and I are beginning a conversation on what we're learning in math class, a pudgy white man with a brown fedora approaches me.

He looks me in my eyes and asks in a tone that makes chills run through my body. "Girl, git up! That seat don't belong to a nigger like you. That's my seat you're sitting in."

I'm thinking to myself when did a seat ever become someone's property? And I am a child. Why is the man treating me as if I am an adult? As I sit in that crusty bus seat, it takes every bit of my strength not to say anything back to this man. While the man starts to get louder, I tune him out and think of Claudette and how she didn't get up from her seat. Claudette stood her ground. I know I can't let anyone treat me like this.

"Excuse me, sir," I say, spitting the words out of my mouth and clenching my teeth into the shape of a smile, hoping he can feel the fire flowing from my mouth like I can.

But as I begin to say something, the lady next to me whispers in my ear, "Baby, pick and choose your battles. I can see you are a strong young woman, but is this the battle you're willing to fight?"

I look around the bus and finally notice that Sandra and the man sitting next to her have already gotten up and taken their seats in the next back row. Pick and choose your battles, I think to myself. 1…2…3 breathe, I tell myself.

As I stand up from the seat, the lady takes my hand, and we walk to the back of the bus together. The lady winks at me and I wink back, tears filling my eyes. Barbara looks at me and mouths the words thank you. I guess this is not the battle I need to choose right now. The battle that I am fighting is helping my sister execute this protest and then getting back home.

Today is the day of the protest! Everyone that is on the team to ensure the success of the protest is in the gymnasium bright and early. Barbara's face is lit up with excitement and a tinge of worry as she reviews everyone's job. The first step of the protest is to lure the principal out of the school.

Two guys on the team pretend they are store owners calling because some Motown students are causing trouble downtown. Luckily the principal takes the bait, leaving us to execute the next step of our plan. From here they deliver fake notes addressed from the principal to the teachers, telling them to bring the students inside the auditorium to make an urgent announcement. While I think it's weird that no teacher actually checked with the principal in person, soon enough students of all ages are filing into the auditorium right and left, the seats so close together everyone is crammed into the room like a pack of sardines.

Barbara is pacing behind the curtain. "Sandy, I'm so scared. There are so many students out there. What if they don't want to protest in fear of getting in trouble? What if they don't want to listen to me? What if…"

"Barbara, don't worry about what ifs," I say. "With some things in life, what-ifs cause you to second guess the ability, the power you have inside you and causes fear to grow inside your core. Don't think about the what ifs. Sometimes you just have to do."

With that Barbara walks confidently to the center of the stage. She takes a deep breath and the curtains open.

When that curtain opened, everyone is awestruck that it is Barbara standing up there on that stage. No one expected her, this shy girl who has never given a speech to this large of an audience in her life, is giving a speech to lead a protest so change can be created in her community. No one expected that power to be stored inside of her and with that power, she convinces everyone to participate in the protest.

We start marching, everyone's voices shout different things, but somehow, we are in harmony. We hold up our signs and march to the beat of our feet with so much power in our feet they sound like drums. We march with power in our voices and wave our signs. We are one unit.

Barbara and I are at the front of the unit leading everyone through the city. The city that doesn't care about their education or success. The city that wants them to learn out of tar shacks instead of brick buildings. The city that wants them to learn out of racial slur-ridden textbooks instead of books that are new and open the doorway to possibility.

We haven't even protested for an hour before the chaos begins... We begin to hear the sound of police and fire truck sirens coming closer and closer towards us. They pull up the trucks and cars to block the road we are marching through. Our unit begins to disassemble. Police officers begin to beat some of Barbara's peers with batons, their screams ringing in our ears, but we continue to march.

White store owners shout racial slurs at us and spit at us, entertained by the harm caused to us, but we continue to march.

They start spraying us with fire hoses to get us off the street and while some people fall down, we still continue to march, not broken by the obstacles people push in our way.

The only thing Barbara and her peers want is a great education. Is that too much to ask? But it apparently is because right at that moment the police cut the dogs loose from their leashes.

"RUN!" Barbara screams and grabbing my hand we take off.

Students sprint in every direction in fear of being bitten by a dog.

I can't believe I honestly thought this protest would differ from the protests in 2020, but it doesn't. Instead of pepper spray and guns, in 1951 they use fire hoses and dogs to dispel Black people off the streets for using our rights of freedom of speech to fight for what we believe.

Barbara and I continue to run, but after ten minutes we finally find an alleyway to sit down and rest.

"Sandra," Barbara whispers, "it doesn't make any sense why they released dogs on us and blasted us with hoses. Our protest was peaceful!"

"I know it doesn't, Barb, but…" I just sigh and hold her hand. I have no words for why people feel threatened by us or why people are afraid of change.

"I love you, Sandy. Thanks for all your help with the protest. I pray that things change." In that moment Barbara pulls me into an embrace. Her hug feels warm and loving.

"I love you too, Barb." While we're hugging, I feel our necklaces rub against each other.

Zaap!

I know what this means.

When I open my eyes, I'm back in the museum again! A loud squeal escapes my mouth!

"I'm back in the museum, I'm back in the museum!" I sing while doing the coolest dance moves.

I immediately speed walk back to my class, but something catches my eye.

The TV is blaring in the museum cafeteria.

I see a Black mom screaming, crying about how they took her son away from her.

The TV switches to the protests and shows people of all colors marching while the police hold tightly to shields as they pepper spray the protesters.

I whisper in tears, "Some things never change."

The Eye of The Stone
by Jennifer Leon, Age 16

It's just another day on the ship. Waking up to the sun on my face, wondering what was blinding me so early in the morning, I got out of bed and looked out my window. I heard the ship horn, loud and noisy. I put on the clothes that I chose yesterday before I went to bed. Then I saw on my shelf my father's necklace. Whenever I looked at it, it made me wonder what he was like. I didn't know anything about him. Not his name, face or even his favorite color. This necklace always made me so curious. It was the only thing I had from him.

Outside my window, I saw a crowd of people heading to the deck of the ship. They were screaming.

"We're here!"

I finished putting on my clothes and left my room as fast as possible. Making my way to the front of the crowd I saw it, the one place that was said to have all the answers: Magnolia City, the place of magic and wonder, where dreams are a possibility. People traveled all over the world just to come here. It was the most beautiful city I had ever seen with buildings of all different sizes. As the sun gazed on the city it looked like a city of diamonds. As the city grew closer and closer, my heart beat faster and faster. With all the problems that trailed me, I knew this was not going to be easy. But

I wasn't gonna let that get my spirits down. I grabbed my camera out of my bag and took a photo of me starting my new adventure.

I spent two weeks in this room bored and impatient. Doing this on my own was hard enough, but I knew deep down it was a journey that I had to do. The struggles I went through just to get here. Thinking about my past made my eyes water. Then I remembered the promise I made to everyone. 'Never lose your smile,' I hear. I wiped my eyes before I could shed a tear and put a smile in its place. I wasn't doing this for myself, I did it for my grandma and all my friends back home. Most of all for my mom. She was the real reason I was on this trip. They made this trip for me to find some answers. And that's what I was going to do: walking forward with a smile holding me together.

Running to the exit of the boat filled me with excitement. As the boat finally docked by the pier, I glided my way through the crowd of people. I saw myself in the streets of Magnolia city. I held on to my backpack tightly and made it through another crowd of people. Grabbing the map I had, I started to see where I needed to head. I had never traveled outside of Angelonia before. Just being here seemed like a fairytale. I couldn't get my eyes to focus. My eyes looked at every little shop, person or plant even though they should be on the map. Observing shops on the street, the people, and the birds that soared in the big blue sky, although it was beautiful, there was something that caught my eye.

I turned the corner and found a flea market. Seeing the whole street filled with signs and goods to buy, I think I have time to explore the streets. I put my map away in my bag. Vendors came up to me, showing off what they had to sell.

"Get your cobbler here!"

"These spices come all the way from Fire Valley."

"These are the finest blades in all the world."

It made me feel like I was home. Our village would have market days like this. When we had market days my mom would always buy me rock candy. She knew it was my favorite. To this day it was still my favorite. It also reminded me of my mom.

I didn't have a lot of memories of my mom. I only had a few moments that I could remember about her. I always had bad memory problems. I got it checked out by the doctors. They described it as amnesia. I sometimes would see flashes of my past. Pieces missing from the whole memory. Ever since I had the accident, I couldn't remember my childhood. The one night that I did remember clearly is the one that haunted me. Flames around my house, blood on my clothes and face, and a gun in my hand.

Thinking back on that, I had to focus on my goal. The whole point of my journey. Walking away from the market I stumbled upon an ice cream store. I looked at the ice cream shop and was amazed. I knew I shouldn't go in, but I couldn't resist. It was like the ice cream was beckoning me. More precisely, it was my stomach. Although I was hungry it occurred to me that I hadn't had ice cream since I was little. My mom would always buy me ice cream. It brought such joy to me.

Entering the shop, I saw all the different kinds of ice cream. Considering what I wanted to buy, I waited in line and as I was deciding on whether to get chocolate thunder or cherry bombs.

Then that all changed when I heard a gunshot.

I turned around to two men who had scars across their eyes. One had a tattoo engraved on his neck and the other had one on his hand. They were both the same style markings. I looked at them and they seemed to be lowly robbers.

"Everyone on the floor right now or you'll end up in your grave," the one with the tattoo on his neck suddenly said.

"Do as he said or he'll make you have an early death," the man beside him said. His voice was raspier than the other man's; he had knives all over his body.

Everyone fell to the floor and listened to his commands.

"This is just sad," I said.

The man with the tattoo on his neck pointed his gun at me. "What'd you say, little girl?" he said with a ponderous tone.

"I said you guys are pathetic."

"What makes you think that? Me and my partner have robbed more places than people to count sheep. I'd watch what you said before you get killed," he said with a hideous grin.

I looked at him and laughed.

"What's so funny?" he said, startled by my laughter.

"I find it hilarious, your big talk. If what you say is true, then why rob an ice cream store? I mean, come on, what kind of criminals rob an ice cream store? It seems to me like you guys are too scared to rob a place bigger than this. I've seen scarier people than you dorks."

Anger spreaded across their faces, ready to start a fight.

The man with the gun exploded. "You little…"

As he pointed the gun at my face, I immediately gripped his hand and made the gun point up. It fired through the roof.

He hesitated as he looked at me, the gun now in my hand. He looked at me and saw me smiling. "Who the hell are you?"

"I'm just a girl who doesn't like guns." I put his gun in my back pocket.

Putting his fist up he throws his punches right and left.

I dodged every attack with ease. I saw his partner from the side. He swung his knife in my direction. I eluded his knife, grabbed his arm and stabbed his partner, who screamed from pain as he drew the knife out from his back. They both looked at me ready to kill me without hesitation.

"Do you guys give up?" I said confidently. While they were both nearly out of breath, thinking about their next move, I looked around to see if anyone was in the way. I watched him carefully for the right moment to strike. As he ran toward me, I saw my opportunity. I ran towards him and punched his face, sending him right towards his partner. Barely having the chance to move he tumbled by his partner and hit the wall.

Then all was still.

I walked towards them and saw them knocked out on the floor. Looking at them, I said, "Idiots." I walked back to the counter and looked for the lady who worked at the store. She was hiding with her hands over her head. "Excuse me, miss? Can I get a cherry bomb with extra chocolate?" I asked her calmly.

Turning towards me she got up and saw that everything was fine. In shock, everyone slowly rose from the ground, relieved that they were safe and unharmed. The lady at the counter gladly gave me my ice cream even with an extra cherry on top. It looked so delicious. I grabbed my ice cream, and reached into my pocket for my money.

"You don't have to pay. It's on the house," the ice cream lady said.

"Really? It's free?"

"Of course, you just saved all of us," she said. "It's the least I can do."

As I turned around, I was smothered by the people in the store.

A girl walked up to me. "Thank you for protecting us. You're like a superhero."

Another woman came up to me and shook my hand.

A man came up. "I've never seen a woman as strong as you. You're incredible!"

This was all too much. I never had this much attention. I felt someone tug on my bag. I looked down on a little girl with ribbons in her hair.

"What's your name, pretty lady?" she asked in such a sweet voice.

I bent down. "My name is Irina Hawkens. What's your name, young lady?"

She looked away shyly. "My name is Alya." She spoke in a soft tone.

I smiled at her and said, "You have a lovely name." I patted her head as she smiled at me. Soon after, everyone wanted my autograph, and I couldn't help but feel a little overwhelmed.

I enjoyed my ice cream after I signed all those autographs. I had never done anything like that before. Happy to help out, I guess. Going outside the store I saw the two criminals handcuffed by police officers. I made eye contact with the one who had the tattoo on his neck. I looked at him and stuck my tongue out.

Walking away from the scene, they got in the car. Then one of the robbers head-butted one officer and knocked him to the floor. He grabbed the police officer's gun and pointed it at me.

"Watch out!" the police officer yelled.

I turned around to see the robber firing the gun at me. I tried to protect myself with my arms and closed my eyes, bracing myself and standing still. I slowly opened my eyes. A man with a sword stood in front of me! I saw the bullet or what I thought was the bullet. I picked it up and saw that it was only half of it. The man had sliced the bullet before it could touch me. I was amazed he had sliced that bullet that fast and at such short range. He was skilled. He was wearing a cloak that had a symbol of a Warrior knight. I had never seen a knight before. They're supposed to be the most powerful people in their nation. I was mesmerized as he spoke to me.

"Are you all right?" he said with a concerned face.

I stuttered and said, "Ye-yes, I'm all right."

He looked at me and smiled. He had such unique eyes. The color was as golden as the sun and his hair was black as the night sky. He walked toward the criminal with his sword to his side. He glared at the robbers. "If you don't want to die here and now, I suggest you give me the gun."

The robber was shaking as he dropped the gun. Without hesitation, he lifted his hands in the air and went quickly into the car. He looked like he was gonna pass out.

"Don't even try to harm innocent people ever again, okay?" said the man with a cheerful face. He lifted the guard and talked to him for a bit.

While they were busy, I got up, making sure that I was fine. Especially my contacts. I lightly touched my eyes and saw that they were still intact. I was relieved that they weren't damaged. If they were, major problems would happen very quickly.

My contacts helped me control my powers. So far I knew I had super strength and healing abilities. I knew I had some other powers, but those were the ones I couldn't control. If they were damaged, the monster that lived inside me would be free. I had these powers ever since the accident when I was eight. My grandmother told me that my eyes would glow white as a pearl. When I wouldn't have my contacts in, she told me, bad stuff would happen. I hadn't known what she meant until I was older. Whenever I didn't have them in, I would feel dizzy and weak. Then I would black out. I couldn't remember what I had done when I woke up. The last time I had lost control, I saw my house on fire. Burning everything in sight, the garden, the house, all of it. I had tried to find my mom. I had blood on my body and I was bruised on my arms and legs. There was a gun in my hand. I didn't know what I had done or what happened, but it was the last time I saw my mother. That was the memory I feared the most. I always believed I was the cause of that. That I had done something awful that made me what I'm today.

A monster.

Examining my contacts, I was relieved that they were not damaged. They were a little fragile, so I always had to be cautious. Looking back at the guy, I knew he was an Ability Wielder like me. He was putting his sword away. I saw a shard in the middle of his sword.

The police officers drove off with the criminals and I got distracted. I didn't see the Ability Wielder walking over to me. I made sure to be careful of anyone who was an Ability Wielder. Since they are illegal, I had to be careful with anyone. My luck is that I got a War Knight. War Knights were the only ones who could have a shard. What I had been told is that most Ability Wielders find people who have shards as threats. I made sure to be cautious. I didn't want anyone to find out about my powers.

He walked over to me. "Hi, my name's Lyon Dagger. It's nice to meet you."

"It's nice to meet you as well," I said, shyly.

He looked at me. "You're not from around here, are you?"

"How can you tell?"

He smirked. "That police officer. He said you just were new here."

"Yes, I arrived today," I said, while avoiding his eyes.

"You're a pretty strong girl," Lyon said.

"It was nothing. I couldn't just stand by and let them get away with their crimes."

"I agree," he said with a smile.

"You're a War Knight aren't you?" I asked.

His smile that shone bright dimmed a bit. He turned away from me. "Yes, I am."

I saw no pride or joy in him. Most Ability Wielders take such pride in their name. What I saw in his eyes was filled with something I too was familiar with: sadness. I quickly changed the topic. "You're from this nation, are you?" I said quickly.

"No, I travel here from time to time. I come from Waterway valley. I arrived today for an urgent meeting. Speaking of which, I must go if I'm gonna be on time. Oh, by the way I never got your name."

"It's Irina."

He smirked. "You have a unique and beautiful name."

I blushed when he started to walk away. I wanted to thank him but was scared to say anything. I don't know what came over me but my mouth spoke for me. "Thank you for saving me," I said.

He stopped for a moment and turned around and smiled. He waved goodbye as he walked off. For an instant, it felt like time froze for me. Like I wasn't a monster inside. Like I was a normal person. I didn't think that I could feel like that. People had always been weird out or concerned. They would stare at me as if something was wrong with me and my strength didn't help. Everyone had always treated me like an outcast, but he looked at me with normal eyes. Not seeing me without a single flaw. I couldn't help but shed a tear. I turned away. I hoped we'd meet again someday.

About five blocks away from the ice cream store I found an Inn called Fire Lotus. It had a cheap room to sleep in for the night. I paid for my room and the lady at the counter escorted me to my room. I gave her a tip and she gave me the key to the room. I opened my room and turned the light switch on. I laid my bags on the floor and plopped myself down on my bed to relax.

"Ow," I said. I grabbed something out of my back pocket. It was the gun. I forgot to give it to the cops. Whoops! I put the gun on the table and laid back on the bed.

I thought about what happened today. I finally arrived at Magnolia City, I toured a flea market, got ice cream, took down two robbers, and I got saved by a War Knight. So much happened in one day. This city never ceased to surprise me. I couldn't wait to see what would happen tomorrow.

I slowly closed my eyes and drifted off to sleep, and back to when I was a child and my mother used to tell me of a magical stone that was given from the skies. She would tuck me in bed and tell me this story all the time. She would always act out the story since she didn't have the money to pay for a book.

"Once upon a time a magical stone came crashing into our world. It shattered in the sky and broke into 100 shards around the world." My mother moves all around my room. "People thought that they were shooting stars but only more magical." She moves her arms up and down.

I giggle when I see her being all weird.

"They became popular in every known nation. People would be amazed by the beauty of the shards. The people soon gave it a name to describe both its value and beauty. They decided to name it Illumiric."

Seeing her write the words in the air makes it seem even more special.

"Overjoyed with a new discovery the people did not know the power at their disposal. By merging the Illumiric shards with jewelry or weapons they saw the power that could be wielded by the shards. People who had the shards were soon known as Ability Wielders. Each wielder was known to have a different power to create, build, heal, fly, and even destroy. Hungry for power, people would fight or even kill for these shards. Soon people started to see the true nature of the power of the Illumiric stone. Bloodshed and slaughters happened in every nation. It was a tragic time for people.

"To stop the chaos a group of people known as the War Knights explored every city to find any Ability Wielder and take their shard. They soon succeeded. And the bloodshed was being put to an end. The people of every nation trusted in the War Knights. The people made a law that any Ability Wielder that doesn›t have the seal of a War Knight will be illegal in every part of the world.

"As the years progressed finding any Ability Wielder was scarce. With each year people stopped believing in the Ability Wielders. None had been seen in such a long time. As for the shards, the War Knights would lock it in a place that no one could ever find, not even members of each nation. They have been gathering the pieces of Illurmic stone for more than 300 years."

"Tell it to me again," I ask her, not wanting her to finish. She starts to walk away. I leave my bed and start to run towards her, but I can't seem to reach her. I yell for her over and over. "Mom!"

Instantly my eyes opened. I found my arm outstretched, but my mother wasn't holding my hand. It seemed that my body had reacted on its own when I was asleep.

I regained my breath and calmed myself down. I brushed the sweat away from my forehead. I needed some fresh air. My mind would calm down after a midnight stroll. I grabbed my room key and left the room. With the door handle in my hand, I looked back at the gun on the table. I grabbed it before I left. Just in case.

Walking out of the hotel, I strolled along the sidewalk thinking about what I dreamt. My mind swarmed with emotions and thoughts. I wanted to forget what I had dreamt. Before I even realized it, I saw a lake. It was beautiful. The stars reflected in the water. I gazed at the water and saw a bench nearby. I decided to rest my mind here. Water had always been soothing to me. I could feel myself starting to relax. Why couldn't I remember my past?

It was something that I wanted to know about myself. I tried my hardest to think about my mom, but I always came up blank. My memories were like a puzzle, and I only had pieces that didn't fit.

Staring at the water, I saw a reflection that wasn't mine. I moved out of range of the bat that had been swinging my way. I found a man with a cigarette in his hand. He was tall and carried a metal bat. I looked at him in shock and wondered what he was doing.

"What's your problem?" I asked.

He grabbed his cigarette and blew out the smoke. "Are you the female who took down two robbers today?"

I look at him confused. "Yeah, I am. What does that have to do with you?"

He blew out another puff. "My name is Axel. Leader of the raven claws. Those two men you beat up were in my crew. So that makes me have a beef with you." He tossed his cigarette away.

I looked at him up and down. I saw a design with something like a tattoo on his neck. It was the same one the robbers had. I got the whole picture. "So, you're here for revenge, right?"

He laughed at me. "I don't care about those fools. No, no, no. I'm not here for that. I'm here for something far greater."

"What do you want from me?" I asked in confusion.

"I want your shard," he said with malicious eyes.

What he said made me very concerned and scared. I knew this wouldn't be an easy fight. "How did you know?" I asked.

"It was quite simple, actually. I had one of my boys visit Vic and Zack in their new home. He told me your strength was something out of the ordinary. But seeing you in person you don't seem that strong. Then it hit me, what if this girl had a certain object to amplify her strength? Something that gives power. To make one person become an Ability Wielder. I knew I had to find this girl because she has something that I want," he said with an evil grin.

"I can take you down all by myself," I said. I got into my fighting stance, ready to pounce.

"Who said I was alone?" Axel said. He lifted his hand in the air and snapped his fingers. Men came from the shadows with weapons—daggers, swords and guns in their hands, ready to fight.

"As if I wasn't busy enough," I mumbled to myself.

"Now how about you hand over your shard like a good little girl, so you don't get hurt?" Axel said.

I was in a tight situation, with at least twenty men or more. I had to come up with a plan to get away from these guys. If I'd had my bag, it would have been easier. I kept gas bombs and my weapons in there for emergencies. Thinking of what to do, I realized something. I still had the gun from the robber in my pocket. I grabbed it before I left my room. Luckily, it still had a full round. The only problem was that I had to deal with all of them. Then their boss. "So, I assume you have as well?" I asked as I slowly reached for the gun.

"Yes, I do actually. And when I have your shard, it will help me become even stronger. I will soon be able to run this city. Nothing will stand in my way."

About to pull the gun, I heard someone speak.

"Well, we can't have that, now, can we?" Lyon said, knocking at least five of Axel's men unconscious. "So, are you the one who's in charge of this little group?" Lyon said in a cunning voice. Lyon made his way through the crowd of men.

"Lyon, what are you doing here?" I shouted.

He saw me in the distance. "What are *you* doing here?"

"I asked first," I said.

"I just got done with my meeting and wanted to chill at my favorite spot and then I heard this man yelling with his foolish scheme," Lyon replied.

"Lyon watch out for the boss, he's an Ability Wielder," I said, back to the situation at hand

Lyon turned his attention to Axel.

"Ah, I see what's going on here. You're a friend of this War Knight. Well, this just got much more interesting," Axel said. "Get them!"

The men started to attack me and Lyon. We fought Axel's henchmen one by one. I started to knock or punch all his henchmen that were attacking me. Lyon had to swiftly strike down all his foes. I saw that he also didn't draw his sword.

"Why the hell are you not using your sword, Lyon?" I yelled.

"I only use this sword when I'm fighting to protect someone. That's the rule when I draw this sword."

Grabbing my gun, I saw that there was a full round. I aimed straight for Axel, who was sitting on a bench. As I pulled the trigger, he smiled at me.

He took his bat and it morphed into a shield. "I guess it's my turn to play." Getting up from the bench he changed the shield into a liquidly substance. It looked like water, but it was covered in silvery metal.

"So, your ability lets you change the shape of your weapon," I said.

Axel walked towards me. "Yes, I can make any metal into any weapon I think of. It's quite useful, wouldn't you say?"

I never knew that an Ability Wielder would be this strong. But I had no choice but to face him.

Axel walked in my direction but was confronted by Lyon. "I think I will deal with your friend before I deal with you," he said.

I didn't know what he was planning, but I rushed over to Lyon to help him fight.

"Oh no you don't," Axel said, sending his liquid metal straight towards me.

The metal attached itself to my body, covered my eyes, arms and legs. I couldn't see or move.

Lyon looked at me. "Irina!" he yelled. He rushed towards me but was confronted by Axel.

"Don't worry, your friend is not going anywhere, but for now you have to deal with me," Axel said.

Lyon unsheathed his sword. "You think you have the skills to defeat a War Knight?"

"We're about to find out," Axel said, as he shaped his metal into dual swords.

I heard them fighting in the distance, with their swords clashing with one another. I couldn't free myself from this metal. The more I moved the more it tightened against my wrists. I didn't know how to get out of this situation. Then I heard it. My contacts were cracking from the metal. I was so scared of what was going to happen. I panicked and called out to Lyon. "Lyon, can you hear me?"

"I'm kinda busy at the moment," he said, dodging attacks from Axel.

"Listen to me. You need to get away from here right now," I said. My contacts were being destroyed by the second. "LEAVE ME AND GET OUT OF HERE," I yelled at him.

"You heard the girl. You might want to listen to her, War Knight," Axel said, grinning at Lyon.

"You're mighty stupid if you think I'm leaving her behind!" Lyon shouted at Axel.

But it was too late. My contacts had shattered as he said those final words. I felt dizzy and unwell. Then all I remembered was my power being unleashed from all the corners of my body. The light from my eyes shone so bright, it broke away the metal that was on my arms and legs like it was nothing.

I turned around and looked at the men. I walked towards them slowly. Out of fear they both stepped back not knowing what was going to happen.

"Irina?" Lyon said.

Axel changed one of his swords into a spear and threw it at me.

Looking at the water from the lake, I commanded it with my mind and used the water to defend myself from the spear. Feeling the pain from my wrist and ankles, I commanded the water to heal my arms and legs. In disbelief, Axel tried again by throwing the sword at me. I grabbed the sword and threw it back. It pinned his shoulder to a building.

"Damn you!" he yelled, agonizing in pain.

I used the water to grab Axel from the wall and brought him closer to me.

"Let me go," he yelled.

I covered his entire body with water, trapping him in a water bubble. I watched him trying to escape and struggling for air.

"Stop, Irina," Lyon yelled. "You're drowning him!"

I dropped him on the floor as he gasped for air. Then I walked slowly towards Lyon.

"Irinia listen to me," he said. "You're safe now. You don't need to fight anymore."

I commanded the water to shape itself into a giant hammer, almost releasing it above Lyon.

"You don't have to be scared, I got you." Lyon's words managed to stop the hammer from raining down.

I lost my balance and started to fall to the ground.

Lyon ran towards me and caught me before I fell and laid me in his arms. "Irina! Can you hear me? Irina?"

Hearing Lyon's voice, I saw him in front of me. In shock, I pushed him away and saw what I had done. Coming to this city was supposed to be a magical and enriching place, but never did I know what problems I would cause here.

The Dragon Chronicles
by Kaya M. Bullard, Age 12

Myths are not stories that are untrue; rather they are tales that don't fit neatly into the historical record, which serves as a foundation to a culture.

-unknown

The Beginning ...

This is a tale of a world where dragons and humans live alike. A world that is drastically different from our own, but also astonishingly similar. If you believe this to be a myth, then you are sadly mistaken, for this is the history of a world millions of lightyears away. The legend of the dragons has been dreamt by many, but for the people of Draconia, this is simply... life. However, before you continue reading, I must warn you. This tale may shatter any and all beliefs you've previously had of dragons.

Still here? Well, I suppose we shall start with how everything came to be ...

How everything came to be ...

Before Draconia, there lived two dragons, Draco and Ania. Draco flew as his massive and strong wings bursted through the stars as if he was showing his dominance with every motion. His scales camouflaged with the darkness of the abyss. While Ania gracefully slithered and slid through the galaxy. Her serpent-like body and scales glowed brighter than the stars. She glided through the air like a graceful air current. With each wave of her tail, you could feel the power and control radiating from her presence. You could recognize Ania's bright graceful beauty from lightyears away, so much so that she caught the eye of Draco. Draco tried as hard as he could to get Ania to love him as much as he did her, he would do anything to have her love. Then finally, with a little bit of charm and persuasion, he somehow succeeded. From that time on, they were always together.

Ten years later, Ania gave birth to seven baby dragons. Era was the oldest with a serpent-like body and ravishing iridescent scales. Similar to her mother, she had a radiant and powerful presence that commanded authority and represented power. Next came Lumi with wings just like her father, her body was white, but her wings were a light turquoise. Out of all of her siblings, Lumi was the most curious.

After Lumi, came Oleander, also with wings. Oleander had a pale brown chest and dark brown scales with a lava undertone. Oleander was calm and collected but also had a sort of arrogance to him. Donner was the middle hatchling with the body of his mother. His scales, similar to Era's, had an iridescent effect with electric blue coloring above, and a brilliant yellow undertone. Donner was extremely playful and energetic and like his older brother, a little arrogant.

Fifth came the one and only Hestia, born with wings and scales that resembled a magnificent phoenix. When she flew it was as though a beautiful flame was dashing past. She was fun and playful but also a bit of a rebel at times. The second youngest was Ampelio. Also with a serpent body, he was the only one out of his siblings who had long luscious emerald dragon hairs that waved behind him. Different shades of green illuminated off his scales. He was definitely on the kinder side compared to his siblings but also a little bit cocky.

And finally, the baby of the seven, Thalassa. She was as gentle as a pond on a calm day but had wings as powerful as a tsunami. When she flew through the galaxies it was like watching the waves crash onto a beach with numerous shades of blue intertwined in her scales.

Ania loved her dragon hatchlings with all her heart!

This made Draco jealous. I must find a way to get rid of them *without* killing them, he thought while he paced through the stars. For Ania would never forgive me if I killed them. But if I simply dispose of them safely, she shouldn't be *that* angry... Yeah... So, Draco flew the galaxy for a suitable planet. It took some time, but he finally found one. This should do. The creatures already inhabiting it shouldn't pose a threat to the hatchlings, and there's a nice warm sun to keep them from freezing. Draco's master plan was in the works.

"Hatchlings!" summoned Draco.

"Yes," the dragons answered as they rushed toward their father.

"Come now. We are taking an adventure, just the eight of us."

"An adventure!?"

"But what about Mamma?" asked Thalassa.

"We are doing this one without Mamma. It's a secret. Are we ready?"

"Yes!" the dragons said with excitement.

"Follow me!"

The dragons flew behind their father, excited to see where he was taking them. They flew through galaxies and billions of stars and planets, but they soon tired.

"Can we rest for a little Father?" asked Oleander visibly out of energy.

Draco, not taking into account the dragon's smaller size, realized they needed rest. "Let's rest on that asteroid over there."

The dragons slept while Draco reviewed his next move.

Once they were all rested, they were on the move again. When they arrived, the destination planet was half land, half water. They flew through the odd planet only to find strange creatures. The most abnormal, yet intriguing, were the creatures with a head and four limbs. Two were for crafting and the others were used for transport and standing (you would call them humans). No color existed! Everything was bland. The water was one shade of dark blue, and the land was a drab gray.

"This is where you wanted to bring us to?" asked Hestia as she tilted her head in confusion.

"Some adventure," commented Ampelio, as he joined his siblings' disappointed expressions.

"Well, you better get used to it, because this is where you will be living for the rest of your lives!" Draco laughed bitterly.

"What!?" Their surprise shook the planet.

"What do you mean, Father? Is this a joke?" asked Lumi, confused and angry.

"No, no children. This is n-" A loud, boisterous, familiar roar interrupted Draco.

They knew they were in *major* trouble.

Ania's body shook all the planets and stars she passed. "Where is my family?" she screamed in rage.

"Well good luck to you guys!" Draco snickered. "This new planet is making my scale's feel weird so I'm off," he said as he struggled to fly away, while the little dragons, still in shock, simply watched. "What is happening to me!? It must be this stupid planet weakening my body! I'm not gonna let this dumb floating pebble stop me!" Draco said. He pushed himself to fly faster.

However, since he wasn't looking forward, he didn't notice the intense meteor shower that was heading right for him. Draco flew from the safety of the unknown planet right into the trajectory of hundreds of humongous comets. Dozens of meteors fired straight for him. Draco froze, petrified. He watched as the large chunks of rock drew closer and closer. When he finally realized what was happening, terror surged through him. His wings shook and flailed in panic! It was as though he forgot how to fly. The massive meteors pierced him anywhere they could. His body, his head, and finally, his wings. He plummeted towards the planet at incredible speed, while the last word he muttered slipped out of his fangs. "How?"

Draco's enormous crash killed half of the planet's native creatures. It also split and scattered half of the planet, creating islands, valleys, and oceans.

For some odd reason, when Draco made contact with the land, it was as if roots of poison coming from the dirt were shot through his body. As if the land was refusing the foreign dragon, but also forcing him towards the ground at the same time. As Draco became one with the land, his deceased body was absorbed into the planet's depths.

Ania and The Seven watched in horror as their love was slowly demolished to pieces. Ania flew to her beloved's remains in disbelief. Almost immediately that gut-wrenching feeling of loss shot through her like a bullet. The very sight of her beloved in this state shattered her heart, almost as if it were made of the most fragile glass in the world. The love of her life, with whom she was going to spend eternity, had just been dismembered right in front of her very eyes.

Ania fell from a hover to the ground, as she bursted into tears. Her radiant, blinding glow dimmed like a dying flashlight. This was an intensely painful sight, so painful it cannot be fully described with words. The Seven joined her, surrounding her.

"Draco!" Ania's screech shook the earth. Large waves rippled over the surrounding waters.

The Seven cried with their mother for days. Their tears fertilized the lands which caused towering trees to erupt from the ground. As their angry, grieving tails struck the rock, the Colossal Mountains formed. The furious steam from their snouts accumulated into the skies which created clouds and rain. The rain brought ponds, lakes, meadows, more trees, and snow. The dragons' grief transformed the bland planet into a beautiful, luscious paradise.

"My children, I cannot stay here," Ania said quietly, as she broke the seemingly never-ending silence.

"Why Mamma?" sniffled Thalassa. She jolted forward.

"Because my darling, I would like to protect you and the planet my true love became one with."

"But how?" asked Ampelio.

"I shall also become one with this land," answered Ania. She moved out of her resting spot. "I will always be watching over you, my children. Take care of the creatures living here for me and your father."

"Wait! Where are you going!?" asked Lumi,

"Don't worry, my child. And remember, I will always be watching over you," Ania said as she gracefully ascended. Her voice faded in the distance.

A bright light illuminated the entire planet. Ania used all her power to transform herself into the atmosphere of the new planet. Ania's atmosphere completed the foundation of the planet as it brightened everything in the process. As the formation of the atmosphere was complete, a burst of dragon magic surged through the land. This granted the humans comprehension of the dragon's language. Ania's soul ascended to the stars and formed the moon.

The Seven hopelessly watched their mother disappear. They felt the dreadful feeling of grief yet again. They struggled to restrain the powerful emotions that surged through them. As a result, their breath trembled at every inhale.

The Seven were the only ones left on the planet, other than the remaining creatures.

"What now?" Hestia broke the silence and erased her sorrow with a single breath.

"Well, Era, you're the oldest. You should be in charge," commented Oleander. He pushed her forward.

The rest of the dragons agreed.

"I guess we should name this planet now that it's ours," said Era.

"Good idea!" said Lumi "What should we name it?" She leaned forward to show her curiosity.

"Donnerland!" said Donner.

"No Donner!" the group disagreed.

"Everyone, think!" Era said.

They thought. But of the many ideas, none were quite right.

"I know!" exclaimed Era. "How about Draconia!"

"Draconia?" asked Donner.

"Like mom and dad's name combined?" asked Oleander.

"I think that's perfect, Era!" said Hestia.

"So, we have all decided," said Era.

"Draconia!" they cheered.

"Now I think we should approach the humans," said Ampelio.

"I don't think that will be that hard," said Oleander. "Look..."

They turned to see the humans hiding curiously behind the newly formed trees.

"Hey!" greeted Donner. He gave the humans a little jump.

"Hello, we come in peace from the stars above," said Era pointing upwards.

The humans looked up to the stars at first confused, but once they understood, they were ecstatic. They whispered to each other, "They from balls of light up there!" They laughed in astonishment. "You lead us?"

"We would like to get to know you guys first! You and the land," explained Era.

The humans nodded.

The Seven flew around the planet and observed the terrain and the geography. They saw that the environments were extremely diverse. One half of the planet had deserts, the other just ocean. One with tall mountains and rock, then another with plain grasslands and luscious meadows. When they returned to the forest, they could finally create a plan.

"So, we've all seen the lands, right?" asked Ampelio.

"We have." They nodded.

"I think the first thing we should do is pick our lands and establish the borders," proposed Era.

"But how are we going to do that if we don't know the exact layout of the land?" asked Ampelio.

"He's right," agreed Donner.

"I'll map out the land real quick!" said Oleander.

"And how exactly are you going to do that?" asked Lumi.

"It's just something I can do," Oleander replied in an almost too casual tone.

He flew as high as he could while he carried a plate of stone in his claws. He drew on the stone with nothing but his talon. He then returned to his siblings with a flawless map of the entire planet.

The dragons blinked in surprise.

"Wha-? How did you...?" stuttered Lumi.

"Like I said, it's just something I can do," said Oleander.

"Okay... There are exactly seven main environments - icy, rocky, one with only clouds, water, forest, desert, and neutral." Era drew a symbol that represented each environment.

"What determines what lands we get?" asked Thalassa.

"I don't know, but it needs to be fa-" Era said.

"You shouldn't determine who gets the lands just yet," a mysterious voice declared.

"Mamma? Wait—where are you?" Oleander asked in shock.

"Yes, it is me. I am speaking to you from above. I strongly advise you dragons not to determine who gets which lands yet. It is not time. When I ascended, I didn't die, I merely became a part of the land to protect you, and with that, I can still communicate with you at times. But I will only do so when I have an important message. Before you choose, there is still one thing remaining that will contribute to the establishment of this planet!" their mother said. "When you were all little hatchlings, I was concerned why you didn't have any powers. But when I took you all to different planets when you were little, I saw that something activated your powers. When I ascended, I altered the land so that you could use them. Before you claim your land you need to discover your powers and where they are strongest. As for what your powers are—just choose the land that calls to you. Good luck…" Ania's voice faded away.

Thalassa was the first to find her powers, in the Draconian Sea, the center of the planet. She was the dragon of the seas. But Lumi's discovery of her powers was the most extraordinary! She was flying around Draconia when she bumped into Hestia, in a rush.

"Hestia!" Lumi yelled as she tried to get her attention.

"Oh, yes?" Hestia said.

"Why are you flying so fast? Are you running from something?"

"Yes, I'm running from that place over there! It is the coldest environment on the whole planet!" Hestia exclaimed. She shivered and her red scales were more pink than scarlet.

"Oh, it can't be that cold, can it?" Lumi said to herself. Hesitantly she flew towards the cold. She was surveying the land when something that resembled a beautiful ice castle caught her eye.

She landed in front of a gigantic, towering ice cave. The entrance was pitch black. Once her claw touched the ice in the cave, a bright, lighted path appeared underneath her. The path thinned into a needle-shaped line and shot forward. The line made sharp turn after sharp turn until it reached its destination.

In the far center of the cave was a tall icicle. It was obvious that it burst through the cave floor. Broken ice was scattered around the perimeter. What rested on the very tip of the icicle, was a smaller, more defined ice crystal. *That* was the line's destination. From the ground, the line revealed the icicle's transparency as it slowly climbed the pedestal and finally reached the crystal. Now the brightest source of light was at the very tip, its sparkle reflected in Lumi's eyes.

Lumi reached her claw out for another touch.

Crack!

"That doesn't sound good." Her voice shook with fear. She heard more. Each louder than the previous one.

Crack! Crack! CRACK!

And then, silence.

"It stopped!" Lumi sighed. But she knew that something was wrong. "It's quiet," she mumbled. "T-too quiet." The volume of her voice steadily increased, as she stepped away from the crystal, panic flooded through her body. But that single step backward was the trigger.

The crystal atop the icicle began to quiver. Faster and faster, it vibrated on its resting point. When suddenly...

Shatter!

The crystal exploded. The tall icicle broke into a million pieces. The absence of the stable icicle forced the ground under Lumi to crack. The cracks formed a kind of circle that surrounded her. She started to shake and rumble with the ground. Lumi dug her claws deeply into the only thing she could. The ice. All was going well.

Until the ice plate underneath her, wasn't there anymore.

She plunged into the darkness! Her wings didn't flap, they flailed in alarm. Lumi watched the only source of light fade, until there was only the sound of her uneasy breathing that notified her that she was still alive.

"No. I won't let go." She took control of her wings and spread them as wide as they could go because she knew this would slow her fall. She used the air collected under her wings to burst upward. She flew faster and faster until she could see the light again. What she didn't notice was that the sharp tips of her wings started to create light trails. Each a different color with every motion she made. Up, yellow. Down, green. Up, purple. Down, orange. She left the cave to fall in the distance as she shot through the cave floor.

The light trails began to expand from the tips of her claws not only out to the distance but through her wings. She no longer needed to flap her wings; she was so high. Lumi paused in mid-air and let the light engulf her body. The colors branched together into one frosty ice blue, almost like the roots of a tree intertwining with each other to meet at her head. The light started to halt as it reached the puny horns on the top of her head. When the light finally reached the tip of her horns, there was a pause.

As Lumi's body sparkled in the faint sunlight, she descended to the ground. As soon as her claw made contact with the snow, the light turned from a slight glitter to a blinding beam. What happened next was similar to a *henshin* you would usually see in an *anime* of some sort. Her small horns grew from tiny stumps into mighty spikes that resembled ice crystals, similar to a flower in a time-lapse video. These translucent spikes also grew at the edges of her wings and gave her a much more intimidating impression. Lumi was now the dragon of snow and ice.

Creatures who were once concealed in the snow came out to bow to Lumi. From creatures as big as yetis to creatures as small as a snow hare and even smaller. The people, who wore newly made hides, also bowed to Lumi. But the most beautiful thing of all wasn't the creatures, it was the magnificent reflection of the aurora borealis from above.

Lumi flew high enough so that every creature could see her. Then, she roared a beautiful yet boisterous roar towards the sky that shook the snow from the trees and mountains. The creatures roared, yelled, and whooped alongside her.

The other dragons eventually found their powers, all in similar ways to Lumi and Thalassa. Era, dragon of the wind, found her powers in the land that was neutral. Oleander, earth dragon, found his powers in the land with the colossal mountains. Donner, dragon of lightning, found his powers in the land of the clouds. Hestia, fire dragon, found her powers in the desert land. And finally, Ampelio, dragon of vegetation, found his powers in the land of the trees.

Now that the dragons discovered their domains, they all met back at Ampelio's domain on the grassy plains.

"We have all found our powers and lands?" asked Era.

They nodded.

"Then we can mark the map with more detail now," Era said. "Oly, can you mark our names where they go?"

"Yup." Oleander added in a few more details he got when he explored the land. "Done!"

"Great! These are our kingdoms. Next, we need to build them," said Era.

"Can we just take a break, Sis! Ever since I discovered my powers, I haven't been feeling so hot," said Donner in a whiny tone.

"Me too," agreed Thalassa, matching Donner's tone.

"I've been feeling that way too," agreed Era.

"Maybe it's this strange planet," said Ampelio.

"It's probably that," agreed Hestia. She rested her hot body on the plain which wilted the grass in return.

The rest of The Seven did the same. Extreme exhaustion rushed through their bodies. They all slowly shut their eyes...

A few weeks passed and the dragons were still in their same spots. During The Seven's long slumber, humans from around Draconia gathered to monitor and check on their beloved dragon leaders. It got to the point where every human in Draconia had set up camp around The Seven's resting area.

"Are you guys all right?" a human finally asked, gently not trying to startle the sleeping dragons.

The humans' speech had definitely improved from the first time they spoke to the dragons.

The first to speak was Era. "W-what-? How long have we been sleeping?" she asked the humans, her voice very raspy and weak.

"A long time," said one of the humans.

"I think the planet's environment is foreign to us. Our bodies are rejecting the entire planet," said Oleander.

"Didn't the same thing happen to Father? Remember before he died he said that the planet was weakening him? What if nothing can be done about this? We might just suffer the same fate," Lumi said with a helpless frown on her face, her light blue scales so pale they appeared white.

The dragons didn't want to admit it, but they knew deep down, Lumi was right. Or so they thought.

"Wait," said Hestia, her frown slowly transforming into an "I have an idea" face. "There might be one way we could live here."

"How?" asked Donner, just as confused as not only the dragons but the humans as well.

"Think about it," said Hestia. "The only creatures that are native to this planet are the humans, animals, fairies, mermaids, and so on."

"So?" asked Ampelio.

"What if we could be native to the land too?" said Hestia. "Like humans."

"And how on Draconia would we do that?" asked Thalassa.

"Must I spell everything out for you guys!?" sighed Hestia "What if we exchange genes with the humans. We could use our magic to combine them!"

"But where would we get each of our genes from?" asked Donner.

"Oh, my stars!" puffed Hestia. "By exchanging blood, Genius!" she said as loud as her weakened body allowed her to.

The idea took a couple seconds for them to absorb, but when everything finally clicked, "Oooohh!" all six dragons said at the same time.

"Ooh!" mocked Hestia.

"You dragons might understand this plan, but we definitely do not," interrupted one of the humans. He tilted his head in confusion.

"Basically, we exchange blood, and our bodies will become more tolerable to this planet, and you guys might become more like us," said Hestia.

"But that's only if you humans agree," Era said.

The humans thought long and hard, but eventually, they decided. "We are okay with exchanging blood with you," they said.

"Yes!" the dragons exclaimed. Their pigment moved up a notch due to their excitement.

"All right, humans! Please organize yourselves into groups by realm," said Donner.

The humans did as he instructed while the dragons drew blood from themselves. Next the humans went up to the dragons and each of them hoped to be chosen by one of them. Each dragon faintly pointed to their chosen human. The chosen humans stepped forward for their blood draw. One noble from each group took a dagger and made a slight cut on the humans' wrists. The chosen ones hovered their wrists just above their dragon's fangs, and let the blood slowly drip into their mouths. Once each dragon swallowed the blood, a bright blinding light shot from each of their bodies. They had all transformed into beautiful humans.

Era's skin was a light brown that glowed in the sunlight, and her eyes were a light grey. Her hair resembled her iridescent scales that shined beautifully in the sunlight; it was long, straight and tucked neatly behind her ears. She had an alluring, gentle smile with adorable dimples near the corners of her mouth and a stare that clearly showed that she was a person of authority.

Lumi was a beautiful darker skinned woman. Her hair was similar to Era's but instead of shiny grey, it was a snow white. Her eyelashes and eyebrows accented her skin perfectly. Her eyes were a nice, almond shape and she had a powerful, strong jawline. Lumi was made even more stunning with her light blue-gray eyes that always had some sort of curious look in them.

Oleander had curly light brown hair, which matched his glowing, sunlight eyes and long eyelashes. He had a calm demeanor but also a slight cocky grin that subtly told you "I know how great I am."

Donner had glowing brown skin, curly, blonde hair, and striking yellow-blue eyes, with lightning that flashed every few seconds inside his iris. Donner had an excited and bright demeanor that made him look really approachable.

Hestia had curly scarlet hair with a fierce gaze and strong warrior body. Her eyes were like no other. She had fire in her eyes, literally. It was as though the colors were constantly changing. From red to orange to blue to purple. She had a fearless, tough, "don't mess with me" kind of appearance at first glance, but when you looked closer, you could see the playfulness in her eyes and the cocky yet appealing grin on her face.

Ampelio had curly, dark green hair that went to about his ears. He also had a bright smile and dimples on his cheeks, like Era. One of his eyes was a vivid green and another was a light brown but both had a kind look in them. His voice was soft yet commanding and similar to his siblings he had a slightly arrogant demeanor.

Thalassa was a tall, beautiful woman. She had caramel skin and her hair was shoulder length and a shiny turquoise. She had stunning ocean eyes, and like her sister Lumi, her eyebrows and eyelashes accented her face. Her smile was also very warm which contributed to her kind and gentle appearance. Thalassa's voice was very soft and gentle, but it was still clear that she was intelligent and tough.

The people were in awe. The foreign creatures that flew from the stars now look just like them. They went from flying, scaly dragons, to beautiful looking humans.

"You said this was an exchange didn't you? What's in it for us?" a human asked, as they stepped forward and broke the silence.

"Right," remembered Donner.

The newly transformed dragons struggled, not accustomed to walking on two legs, to their stored blood.

The humans got back into their groups while the dragons served them cups of blood. Some humans received seven cups, while some received four. The chosen humans got seven, while everyone else got a random amount. It all depended on their place in the line.

The humans scrunched their faces at the taste. A similar glow from the dragon's transformation happened when the humans drank the blood. They turned into mini versions of The Seven. They energetically flew around in circles and loops with their new powers. Hestia's small dragon whipped fire from her tail which caused the grass of the plain to catch on fire. Immediately,

Thalassa's small dragon extinguished it with a mist of water by flapping her wings. The humans that received less blood, had less of a transformation but still had powers.

There were dragons that flipped and flew through the skies and humans played with their new skills on the ground. Smiles shone across every face, including the dragons.

"Wait!" yelled Hestia. "What is it? Do our powers work even if we're not dragons?" she asked. She stepped away from her siblings and then WOOSH! She blew a huge ball of fire from her fist.

"Was that really necessary?" asked Donner while he shrugged.

"Ya, you could've just flicked a little flame on your finger, but you decided to set the whole plain on fire," said Thalassa, as she put the fire out with an even bigger wave of water.

"Now look at what you've done! The plane is drenched!" yelled Ampelio. He touched the ground which made glistening green grass shoot from the ground.

"You guys need to stop!" Era laughed.

The Seven laughed with her.

But suddenly, dragons started to drop from the air!

"What's going on!?" Thalassa yelled.

What they hadn't noticed was that behind them a bright, white light rose from the ground. They turned around.

"Mom!?" the dragons said together in shock.

"Do you know what's going on?" Lumi asked.

"I do. Just like how you guys became weak when you were dragons for too long, if the humans are in their dragon form for too long then they will become very weak," said Ania.

"Wait! Dragon form? What do you mean dragon form?" asked Hestia.

"You haven't fully transformed from dragons to humans, and they haven't fully transformed from humans to dragons either. All you've done is create another body for yourselves and the humans," their mother said.

"You're saying we have two bodies now?" asked Ampelio.

"Yes, Ampelio my sweet."

"But how do we get back?" Oleander asked, extremely confused.

"You simply imagine yourself in your desired form."

The dragons obeyed, then quickly changed back.

"Is it the same for humans to?" asked Era.

"Yes. All they have to do is imagine themselves back in their original body," said Ania.

Almost immediately, The Seven went to tell the fallen dragons how to become human again.

Luckily the humans understood and quickly returned to their original human form.

"Thank you, Mamma," Donner said.

"Of course, my darling. Now for the true reason I'm back. I came to congratulate you on your accomplishments. You are now ready to build your empire. I am so proud of you, and I wish you the best of luck," Ania said as her voice ascended back up to the moon.

"Oh ya! We did it," remembered Lumi.

"We better get started. We've got a lot of work to do!" said Donner.

"Yes, but we have to promise to continue to work together. Okay?" said Era.

"All right. I vow to keep working together," they said in unison.

They changed into their dragon forms and flew to their realms. Their people followed them...

A few years later, and the dragons ruled their prosperous, powerful empire with love, care, and passion. They kept their vow and built the Draconia capitol where the original blood exchange took place. The capitol was an architectural feat! The Seven met there every month and it was the center of the world. Statues of The Seven, in their dragon form, were perched on the perimeter of the building. But that was the second sight after the two-thousand-foot star needle that towered over the entire capitol.

Each dragon had their own palace. Some of them were in plain sight like Hestia's palace of fire, or better known as The Red Palace, with beautiful crimson crystals that formed the outer walls of the gigantic fortress, while others were very well hidden, like Donner's castle of the clouds. When within 100 miles of his castle a large thunderstorm would suddenly appear, visitors caught in the eye of the storm had to catch the lightning train. The train would flash through the storm clouds and make sure to slow down so that any passenger onboard the train could see the golden lightning palace in all its glory. The Seven weren't the only ones living lavishly. There was no poverty in all of Draconia. Everyone at least had a small cottage; The Seven made sure of that.

All was good in Draconia. They held their annual Founders Day Festival, the biggest of the year, where anyone who wished could travel to the capital and celebrate with anybody, no matter the status, that included The Seven. They were having a ball, just like every year, when suddenly, BOOM! Everything froze. There was a deadly silence until ...

"The Capitol!" one person yelled and pointed.

The citizens' pride and joy, the most significant building in all of Draconia was just destroyed.

"Noooo!" some yelled.

Others started to weep, others fell to the ground in disbelief, while most of them were just confused.

But The Seven...

The Seven were frozen.

Petrified.

Blood in the Snow
by Mackenzie Bell, Age 14

Sierra

The snow fell heavily from the inky sky. Everyone was bundled up in the warm comforts of their home, celebrating the holidays with their families. All except for one.

Spraying snow in the air, Sierra sprinted through the newly made winter wonderland. At least it would be a wonderland if James Mickey had still been alive. Blood rolled off her fingertips and the sleeves of her soiled jacket. She threw it in the trash, a giddy smile covering her cold face. She had to do this. It got her heart pounding, blood rushing. Sirens blared loudly around her. She picked up speed, but it was too late. A black police car swerved in front of her, and a scrawny policeman leapt out of the car. He was young and scared, his gun shaking in his hands as he pointed it at her. She couldn't get caught now. She couldn't leave her sister alone like this. She gave the officer a sweet, warm smile. As sweet as someone covered in blood could give. She raised her hands in the air as if she were surrendering. In reality, she was watching, waiting, studying the officer for any sign of weakness. There it was! As quick as a fish leaping down a stream, she saw the flash of uncertainty and confusion in the officer's eyes. She launched at him and...

"Helloooo Sierra, are you alive?"

Sierra gasped, looking around wildly. She found herself in an office, stacked high with books and posters. Before she could truly wake up a familiar voice shook her out of her haze.

Her sister, Mal. She stood in front of her, the police badge on her chest catching the sunlight. "Man, you really have to stop dozing off in here. My colleagues think you're a hobo!"

Sierra wiped the remaining drool off her chin and smirked. "Who cares what they think? You know all your colleagues are stuck-up!"

Mal scoffed, almost as if she was offended. "Not *all* of them are like that!"

"Oh yeah, name one who isn't!"

Mal opened her mouth then paused, seemingly stumped. "Whatever! That's not the point. The point is, you cannot doze off here anymore," Mal said, while slinging her purse over her shoulder, and turning to leave. "You're disrupting my workspace!"

Sierra sighed and followed her out of the door. "I know, I know, I'm sorry, sis," she said half-heartedly. "Won't happen again."

Mal looked over at her with squinted eyes. That was her analyzing look. Sierra hated it. "Why are you so tired anyway? You know, I can never seem to find you in the evenings, where do you go?"

Sierra froze, trying her best to keep her cool. She scratched her wrist. That always seemed to calm her. "Whoa, are you like my babysitter now?" she joked. "I go where the wind takes me, sis."

Mal gave her a look, but Sierra's answer seemed to satisfy her for now. "Whatever you say, Sierra," she said. She pressed the button to the elevator.

Sierra held in a sigh of relief as the elevator doors opened. Mal was always prying, always concerned about her. She loved her for it, but it was going to get them both in trouble one day. Sierra had to be more careful about going out now. She pressed their floor button and thought about her new "assignment" on the way down. A young woman by the name of Cheri. What a pretty name.

She was so busy thinking about her strategy, she barely heard her sister's question.

"Can I "ride the wind" with you tonight?"

Panic gripped Sierra like ice. Her sister wanted to come *with* her? Why? Mal was always so busy with work, always so responsible about going to bed and getting up on time. Did she suspect something? Only then did Sierra realize that she looked weird just staring at her sister and panicking quietly. "Uhm—why? Don't you have to go to work tomorrow?" she asked, trying to remind her sister of her duties.

"Well yes, but I've been meaning to take a break. This job can get really hectic. We don't have to stay out too late, but I thought it would be fun," Mal replied with a smile. "I also wanted to spend some time with you. It's been a while since we've just hung out, you know?"

Ugh. Now Sierra felt guilty. Mal was right, it had been a very long time. She thought for a while weighing her options carefully. Should she risk getting caught by her sister? How would she even react? Sierra sighed. Neither of her options were good. "Let me think about it?" she said as she stepped out of the elevator.

Mal shrugged. "Okay, you hungry?" she queried.

Sierra smiled and nodded, pleased that her sister accepted her answer without many questions.

Later that day Sierra sat alone upstairs in her room. She scrolled absently through her phone. It was going to get dark soon, the perfect time to carry out her "assignment." It's best to do these things at night. She pondered her sister's offer, the thought circling through her head. Maybe she should bring her along? Maybe she could even tell her about what she really did at night?

No!

Just as the thought crossed her mind, the darkness swarmed around her. It suffocated her, enclosed her mind and thoughts. That darkness had always been there, even when she was just a child. It clouded her vision and her judgement. It whispered in her ears, urged her to bend to its every whim. She could never rid herself of it, never resist its call. She hated the darkness but listened to it every time.

You can't tell her.
What about everything we've worked for?
Don't be an idiot.
You will go alone and carry out your assignment.

It was gone just as fast as it took hold of her. Sierra rubbed her eyes frantically. Tears pricked her eyes. She stood up and silently gathered her backpack and put on her clothes. After taking a deep breath and collecting herself, she stepped out of her room to confront her sister.

Mal was lounging on the couch watching TV. When Mal saw her coming, she smiled at her cheekily. "Hey sis!" She seemed to notice her somber expression and her face fell. "Whoa, are you okay?"

Mal's concern made Sierra's heart ache. Would you still care about me if you knew what I've done? Sierra shook the thoughts out of her head, feeling the darkness that crept back into her mind. She forced herself to put on the mask of emotion she did every time. "Of course, I'm fine! I just wanted to tell you I think I have to go out solo tonight, I'm sorry." Mal made that face again, squinted eyes, furrowed brows. Like she was really concentrating. Sierra always felt those cool blue eyes start to crack at the mask she spent so many years of her life perfecting. She hated that expression.

"Why do you have to go out alone tonight?" Mal asked, the hint of suspicion clear in her voice.

Sierra stiffened, feeling a bit defensive. "Why do you always have to know where I'm going? I don't need someone to babysit me. I'm a grown woman," she spat.

Mal didn't bat an eye, simply narrowing her eyes more. She didn't respond, just sat there glaring silently. Sierra felt as if she could drown in the tension. Finally, her sister shrugged, and turned back to the TV. "Okay, have fun," she said dismissively and watched her show like nothing had happened.

Sierra was confused but didn't question and hurried back to get the rest of her stuff. As she hurried out the door, her sister barely looked at her and just waved. Wow, that was easy. A little too easy. She walked faster, brushing off her unease as she made her way deeper into the city and closer to her target. The darkness surrounded her again, guided her through the dwindling crowd of people. The darkness didn't see anyone as real people, just moving sacks of flesh. The world around faded to fuzzy shapes as she slipped on her mask, and fully slipped into the dark. It was so loud and unrelenting; she couldn't see who she was looking for. She looked around until she saw a fire escape by a towering apartment building. Perfect. She darted over, trying her best to stay in the shadows and climbed up the ladder quickly. She surveyed the world below her, trying to find her target through the noise. All of a sudden, a bright, red fire blazed through the static. She squinted trying to make out the shape and realized with a start that it was her sister!

Why is she here? Is she following me? Does she see me? Does she know? Panic flooded through her veins and turned her blood to ice. She stiffened, almost losing her footing on the roof. She backed away quickly, breathing hard. She waited a moment, trying to get herself to relax. She just had to be more careful is all. There's no way she saw me. Sierra crept back slowly towards the edge of the rooftop and sat on it. She took a deep breath and looked down again, only to see her sister's blue eyes looking right back. Those sharp, blue eyes, piercing through the darkness and tearing down her mask. Common sense told her to move back, to hide, but she couldn't. She was stuck staring at those ocean eyes.

Her sister then calmly turned and started walking towards the building.

That's when Sierra's gears started turning and she snapped back into life. She ran towards the side of the building and effortlessly leapt to the next rooftop; she had escaped this way before. As she leapt away her mind ran rampant with thoughts. But one voice trumped all the rest, loud and clear.

Two can play at that game.

Sierra leapt from building to building without looking back. She found a staircase on one of them and ran down quickly, out of breath. Great, now she had to do this with her sister snooping around. She would have to lose her. She stepped out the building's front door and looked around. Sierra was already down the street. She rounded the corner and sprinted away, looking behind her for any signs of her sister. And crashed right into a young woman.

"Oh! I'm sorry, I wasn't paying attent..." Her words failed her as she saw who she'd ran into.

Cheri, her newest victim.

"It's all right!" Cheri said with a cheerful expression. She walked away.

Sierra watched her walk, hunger gleaming in her eyes. The dark swooped over her once more, turning Cheri into a bright green shape. She followed the girl slowly, trying her best to seem invisible. She was so enraptured by her target that she completely forgot her sister was still in the area. The girl turned a few corners before nearing a small apartment building.

She couldn't let her get inside, then she would be too late! Sierra quickly looked around her surroundings and saw a small alleyway close to Cheri's apartment. Perfect. She pulled her hood over her head and made her move, grabbing Cheri and covering her mouth. Cheri screamed against her hand and struggled aggressively, but she wasn't as strong as her. Sierra dragged her, kicking and screaming to the alleyway, and pulled her into the darkness. She wondered if Cheri got a small taste of what she was consumed with almost every day. Nobody could fully understand what she went through. The cold, unrelenting dark. It never let her go. It was insatiable. Suddenly the noises got so much louder, the static so much thicker. Her vision went out completely and the last thing she remembered was the sound of muffled screams, and the thick smell of blood.

Mal

Mal stopped running. She put her hands on her knees to catch her breath. She had been running all over the city looking for her sister, until she saw Sierra sitting on that building. When she got to the roof her sister had disappeared into thin air. Mal assumed she somehow climbed down the side or went rooftop jumping. Why would she need to do that? How does she even know how to do that? Something was wrong with her sister; she could see that much. Sierra acted so suspicious, Mal just couldn't figure out what was going on. Could her sister really be doing illegal stuff?

Mal sighed and kept walking, nearing an apartment building. Just as she was pulling her phone out to call Sierra, she noticed an odd scent in the air. A smell she dreaded but had no choice to ignore as a police officer. It smelled like blood. It came from a dark apartment building. She narrowed her eyes and let her hand rest on her knife that she never left home without. She walked to the back of the dark alley. Her boots splashed in something. She looked down and her heart caught in her throat. At her feet lay a mangled body, face down in the dirt. She called her department and they collected and identified it.

The next day, Mal came home to find her sister in the kitchen making breakfast.

Sierra smiled at her shakily. "Good morning, you want some pancakes?"

Mal accepted and sat down with her sister to eat. "Did you hear about that murder last night?" she asked her, analyzing her quietly. She noticed her sister scratching her wrist, looking somewhat nervous.

"No, I didn't. That a case you're working on?" Sierra asked.

"Yeah, you can say that. It was kind of close to us."

Sierra's nails dug in deeper. "Well thanks for telling me, I'll be more careful," she said, smiling at her.

"Yeah—careful," Mal said, almost to herself and finished eating pancakes with her in silence. She watched her sister get up and finish getting ready for work.

"Hey, have you seen my bracelet?" Sierra asked.

"No, I don't think I have."

Sierra shrugged. She grabbed her purse and left for work anyway.

Once her sister was out the door, Mal reached in her pocket and pulled out some slightly stained jewelry. She leaned over it. A few hot tears slid down her face and stained the jewel more.

She had neglected to tell her sister she found her blood-soaked bracelet by the body.

She held the bracelet close to her chest and cried, sobs wracking her body over and over again. Her mind was a cacophony of emotions, mostly confusion and fear. Last night, after she'd found the bracelet, she hadn't been able to process anything. She had stood in the shower for hours, not even cleaning herself, just trying to get the water to wash away all her thoughts. It hadn't worked.

When she got out, she just sat in her bed, in complete denial. Her sister couldn't be a murderer. She just couldn't. After everything they'd been through, the things they'd suffered. Sierra couldn't be like all the people who had hurt them in the past. Maybe it was someone else's bracelet? It wasn't really special. It wasn't until this morning when she saw how nervous Sierra was, looking for her bracelet—that's what finally shook her out of her denial.

She didn't know what to do, should she turn her in? It was her job after all, but what other proof did she have besides this bracelet that could belong to anyone? The police couldn't find any fingerprints or evidence that would point to a suspect. The thought made her sick to her stomach, not only was her sister a murderer, but she was also an experienced one at that. She quickly jolted herself out of her thoughts and sighed. She would end up late to work soon. Mal wiped her tears and turned the bracelet around in her hand. Another thing to worry about: she broke the law by stealing evidence from an active crime scene. She glared at the bracelet and got up to shove it in her nightstand. She would have to deal with that later. For now, she had a job to do.

Sierra

Sierra leaned back in her seat and turned up the radio in her car. She had just pulled off another successful "mission," but all she felt was unease and trepidation. She couldn't enjoy her victory when she knew her sister had seen what she'd done. Even if Mal didn't know it was her, she still felt bad for subjecting her sister to her mess. She wondered for like the 1000th time what might happen if she confessed to what she's done. Just as the thought crossed her mind the shadows started to claw at the edges of her mind again, reminding her what a monster she was.

"I know, I know, you can't tell anyone, blah blah blah." She growled to no one in particular. "Just shut up already, Kage" she said, her voice breaking just a bit. She had decided to name the shadow in her head, tired of just calling it "the darkness." Kage meant "Shadow" in Japanese. She thought about how fitting that name was as she pulled up to her job at the gym. She strolled in, greeted by the familiar smell of rubber and sweat. The smell and sounds of the equipment calmed her nerves, until she looked up at the TV. Her heart dropped into her stomach as the news reporter recounted the events of the murder last night.

"Pretty scary huh?"

She whirled around as she heard a loud voice behind her. One of her colleagues, who she wasn't really close to. He seemed to be too engrossed in the news story to notice her distress.

"What?" she asked, slightly irritated.

"The murders," he continued casually. "Pretty scary right? Right in this area too."

Sierra shuffled uncomfortably. "Yeah, I guess so," she mumbled.

"Says that she got stabbed ten times! Can you imagine? How crazy do you have to be to take it that far?"

The words swirled around her and only increased her unease. She'd seen some of her work on the news before. It usually gave her a smug sense of pride, watching people scramble to unearth her identity. Why was it bothering her so much today? Deep down, she knew why. She could only imagine her sister as one of those people. Working so hard to solve the case, taking extra shifts and burning herself out. She knew how her sister felt about criminals, especially those who murder without reason. She hated them. Saw them as barbaric, unfeeling, monsters. Just like her. Any other day she would argue that she *did* have a reason. That Kage and her terrible childhood drove her to these murders. Who was she kidding? She shared that childhood with Mal and she was an amazing person and officer. She could've gotten help to get rid of Kage or told her sister before it was too late. Instead, she'd let Kage drive her to insanity.

Sierra turned on her heels and stormed out the door. Tears clouded her vision. Her breathing came in short bursts that she knew weren't very healthy as she stomped down the street. She didn't know where she was going or why she felt this way, she just knew she had to get out. Suddenly her vision started to fade into black. She panicked. Why is this happening now? Her tears fell as she was surrounded by the dark.

Mal

Mal had started to get worried. She could barely focus on work, so she got off a bit early. When she got back her sister wasn't home. Her shift should have been over by now. A chill went down her spine as her thoughts went back to the bracelet she left in her drawer. Could Sierra have found it? She ran into her bedroom to check and sure enough, it was still there. Relief and confusion came over Mal. If Sierra hadn't found the bracelet, why wasn't she home? Could she be hurting people? Mal shook the thoughts out of her head. Her sister had just done that yesterday; she wasn't likely to do it again that soon. She had been watching the patterns of the murders, they were quite random, but they never happened multiple times a week. She breathed a sigh of relief and put her shoes back on. She wasn't just going to let her sister run wild though. As she got ready, she looked at her gun on the table.

Hesitantly, she grabbed it and put it in her holster. Where are you, sis?

Sierra

Sierra couldn't believe this. One second she was at work, the next there was someone laying at her feet, bleeding. He wasn't dead, but he wasn't looking so good either. She stared at him blankly as he tried to get to his feet to no avail. He would die soon if she didn't *do* something, but she couldn't. She would forever be a monster. She snapped out of her thoughts when she heard the loud sound of a car door closing. How had she not heard the car come up?

The man heard it too and cried out for help.

Fear of being caught, ironically made her freeze. She might have to fight her way out of this. She heard heavy footsteps turn the corner and...

Her sister stared back at her.

Sierra felt herself panic. Out of all the police officers, out of all the people, Mal found her first. Her sister's eyes widened as she looked between the body on the ground and her. Sierra began to spiral. Mal would yell at her and arrest her and look at her with repulsion through prison bars, every time she went to work. She didn't expect Mal to give her that sad, soft look she used to give her when they were kids, and Sierra was crying in the corner.

Mal sighed and pinched her nose between her fingers. "Sierra just... come on."

Shock rattled her. "What? What do you mean come on? What about the guy?" Sierra looked down at him. He was leaning against a wall. He had managed to use his jacket to cover his wounds to slow the bleedings. He looked at her with a mixture of anger and fear.

"Just leave him."

Sierra and the guy look equally shocked by her words.

"L-Leave him?" Sierra stuttered. "Mal, you realize I did this right? I almost killed him. He'll die!"

The man curled up at these words, accepting his fate. He didn't really speak much.

"I know you did this, Sierra. I also know that you stabbed that lady last night. I know that you've killed several people."

Sierra took a step back.

"You left your bracelet on her body."

Sierra cursed herself silently. She'd never made a mistake like that before. "Why aren't you mad? Aren't you going to take me to jail?" she asked.

Mal sighed. She looked so guilty and small now, not at all like the headstrong woman Sierra had known her whole life. "No," she said quietly. "I can't lose you. I don't have any family left."

Sierra looked down at her feet. Neither did she, it had just been the two of them for the longest time.

"I can offer you a way out."

Sierra's head snapped up. "What?"

"A way out," Mal repeated. "You don't have to go to jail, sis. I'll cover for you. We can get you some help. We can—figure it out."

Sierra looked at her sister with shock. All she had wanted for the longest time was some help. A way to clear the voices from her head. Her sister was offering that right now yet...

"Please, Sierra?" Mal reached her hand out for her.

Sierra still couldn't let go. She wanted to take Mal's hand and leave but some part of her was still unsure. "I don't know Mal, what if I can never get better? I'm just a monster now," she said while taking another step back.

Her sister took a step forward. "You don't have to be! You can be better. I can help you. Just take my hand."

Sierra took a few steps forward. She probably looked like a stray cat being coaxed out of the shadows by some food.

Her sister gave her a shaky smile and stuck her hand out further. Just as she was about to grab it.

Stop.

Sierra yanked her hand back and grabbed her head. She heard her sister's voice at the edges of her mind, sounding concerned. She could barely focus on that because Kage's voice was so incredibly loud. She felt a hand on her shoulder and her head snapped up. Her heart dropped at what she saw. It wasn't her sister standing there anymore. It was *him!* With his sickeningly wide grin and shadowy face. How was this possible? She hated him, all the pain and suffering he'd caused her and everyone around her. She lost so many friends and family members because of him. Every time she would try to connect to someone or reach out, he was always standing there. Blocking the way or steering her away from any good in the world. Now here he was, shaking her shoulders and mocking her with that stupid grin, and that awful noise. But this would be the last time she would let him stand in the way of people she loved. She glared up at him and shoved him back.

He tilted his head in confusion, but that awful expression never changed.

"I hate you," she hissed at him through clenched teeth. Then she pounced at him, knife in hand.

Sierra plopped down on the ground, breathing hard. The knife hit the ground with a loud clatter. It was over. The monster was gone. She crawled towards the man behind her and shook him gently. No reaction. He was long gone already. She frowned and gently closed his eyes. "I'm sorry. I hope your family finds you," she said softly. She thought about Kage and what to do with his body. Was Kage even human?

She turned around to survey the damage and then stopped. Her heart crawled up her throat and her stomach turned. She could barely suppress the urge to throw up. Kage was gone, and her sister's lifeless eyes stared back at her.

I'll Always Be Here.
I Am You.

The Magic of Ms. Magissa: Helen's Hair

by Mariah McCoy, Age 14

Proof. What is proof? My definition was not nearly as difficult as Ms. Magissa's. Whoa...I'm getting a little ahead of myself. Let's start on a simpler subject, like my name. My name is Aurelie Sagacita. My journey began the first week of school. It was my first day at Doctrina Bona High School. It was also Career Day, where we were asked to dress in the attire of our future careers.

I gazed into the mirror at the sharp, mint green suit I borrowed from my mom. I plan to start my own business one day, so I dressed as an entrepreneur. I fixed the collar, so it sat neatly on my defined collarbone. "Aurelie Sagacita, CEO of Sagacita Enterprises," I said to my reflection. I imagined my future self representing my own business.

The knock on my door interrupted my reverie. My family stood huddled in the doorway. My dad clutched his polaroid camera tightly to his chest, poised to lift it at any moment.

"Wow, you look just like your mother!" my dad exclaimed as my mom came over to lay my baby hairs.

I've been told before I am the spitting image of my mother—same defined cheekbones, same dark, mysterious eyes, and the same plump, rosy lips. Standing next to her in the mirror, this statement finally made sense to me.

"Picture time!" my dad said as he tried to hide his sad expression. This was our first picture without my sister, Monerica, who had left for college. A millisecond before my dad snapped the camera, my phone crooned the iconic hook from "Can You Stand the Rain" by Boyz II Men.

"Monerica!" I shrieked with excitement. We all squeezed into the tiny FaceTime box as I answered my sister's anticipated call.

"Hey everyone!" she exclaimed, smiling from ear to ear.

After we said our greetings and she explained everything she loved about NYU, she asked: "Aurelie, which teachers do you have?"

I whipped out my schedule and read: "Carter, Phillips, Magissa, McC--"

"Magissa?" she interrupted. "She's probably the worst teacher there. She tends to contradict herself a lot. But, as long as you don't challenge her on anything, you'll get a decent grade. She is not the type of teacher who accepts criticism very well."

I have a history of being vocal. I am never disrespectful, but I politely ask teachers to explain something that doesn't align with what my parents have taught me from a young age. Sometimes my teachers have agreed with me, and sometimes I change my viewpoint on the topic. I consider it a learning experience.

"Aurelie will form her own opinions, Monerica. Just because you didn't like Ms. Magissa doesn't mean your sister won't," my mom said.

I walked into school later that morning with an optimistic attitude, despite what my sister said. Today was going to be a good day.

As I sat in my seat waiting for the final bell to ring, I scanned the classroom. A portrait to my left immediately caught my eye. It was an intricate painting of a woman with tanned skin, pecan eyes, and flowing auburn hair. She was very majestic. There was even an aura around her. The flames that surrounded her on every side stopped just short of her, as if she was untouchable. I squinted to read the writing on the bottom: Helen of Troy. *Helen of Troy? Didn't she have blonde hair?*

"Good morning, class!" Ms. Magissa exclaimed.

"Good morning Ms. Magissa!" I replied, as bubbly as possible. About 36 heads whipped around in my direction. I shifted nervously in my chair. *Was it not customary to respond?* I tried to ignore my classmates and turned my attention to my new teacher. She looked very whimsical and disheveled. Her eyes were two different colors: one red, one blue. Her red eye must have been made of glass, because it was never in sync with her Carolina Blue one. Her salt-and-pepper hair was visibly matted and untamed, even though she'd obviously attempted to masque it with a vibrant headband, which in no way matched with her pink kimono with giant sunflowers.

"Welcome to Art! Oops!" She rolled one eye. "I mean welcome to History. Art is intertwined with History, and everything is art, so why not?... Anyway, my dream job was to paint. One night in the cave, I told my family that I aspired to be an artist. And what did they do? They *laughed* at me. 'Docinda, your art is hideous,' my dad used to say. 'Your sisters are teachers so you should be too. You're all the same person anyway.' So, I became a teacher and have wasted the last few centuries with ungrateful urchins like yourselves. Thanks a lot, Dad. I love being a triplet!"

An awkward silence descended on the room. Then, after a few seconds, a sound escaped Ms. Magissa's mouth. At first, I thought she was choking, but then she started smiling. *Is she... laughing?*

"I'm just kidding," she got out, in between spurts of snorting. "Do I look like I've lived for centuries?" Before any of us could answer, she started mumbling to herself. Just when the moment got fully awkward, she suddenly clapped her hands. "Time for a little game!" She flipped open her notebook. "Now, don't think of this as a quiz. This is just an assessment of knowledge," she explained. "I don't expect you little urchins to get anything right anyway," she added under her breath.

"Let's do it!" I said happily.

Ms. Magissa's eye shot up from her page. "There will be no room for sarcasm in this class," she said ominously.

My sister always told me that first impressions are everything, but Ms. Magissa's glare was making me wish I could take back my words. But I've learned that words are like mist from a perfume bottle—they never go back in. "No disrespect intended, Ms. Magissa. History just really excites me!"

Ms. Magissa searched my face for any signs of humor. When she saw I was serious, her face lit up. "Oh! Thank you for your enthusiasm." She turned her attention to the class. "Who won the Trojan War?" she asked.

"The Greek army," I blurted out. I just got a book for my birthday that spotlights all important moments in history, and I must've read it ten times, at least. *At least.*

"Correct," Ms. Magissa exclaimed. "I guess that was too easy. Here's the next one: What color was Helen of Troy's hair?"

That's oddly specific.

"Blonde," I offered.

"Are you sure about that, Aurelie?" A yellow-toothed smile bloomed on her face.

I would hate to be her dentist.

"Yes ma'am," I asserted.

She eased toward my seat with a new sparkle in her eye. "How can you prove that your answer is true?" she asked. She was hovering inches away from my face.

So much for personal space! A foul smell insulted my nose. Her perfume smelled of dead roses, or like it had expired years ago. I also might need to get my eyes checked because those sunflowers on her kimono seemed to be swaying. I struggled to collect myself before I spoke. "Well... I can't prove anything... so I don't really know how to answer your question." The odor was starting to give me a headache. "I guess I know nothing for sure, but I read a very informative book this summer. The picture of Helen in the book showed her with beautiful blonde hair."

"That answer was extremely... cold. Too icy for my liking. Print is not proof, Aurelie. Come back when you have some."

"Wha--" Before I could ask what she meant by "proof," my vision went black. I was sure my eyes were still open, but I couldn't see anything. Suddenly, I was rising from my seat. I desperately clung to my desk to prevent my ascension, but it was no use. Before I knew it, I was outside in the summer sun. Even through my thick blazer, I could feel the warm rays. My body rocketed me toward the sky as my vision returned. It felt like I was being fastened into an invisible roller coaster. I was racing at around 100 miles per hour. *This is crazy.* I had never gone this fast. I felt nauseous from the speed.

Suddenly the ride dropped me on sand. I was on a beach.

Maybe Ms. Magissa placed a virtual reality set on my head. *Wow, these things are very descriptive.* It was like I was really on a beach! I felt around my eyes and the back of my head in order to pull the headset off, but nothing was there except... a new hairstyle! I marveled at the intricate updo in my head, that weaved in and out like a basket. I traced my finger around my head like a maze, finding no end to the intertwining braids. *How did this get here if my hair was out, 30 seconds ago?*

"Ms. Magissa?" I called out to no one. "This isn't funny!"

To my right was a cluster of shacks, in the distance I could just see a great wall, and to my left, colossal wooden ships waded slowly in a wine-dark sea. I zeroed in on a particular ship in the water. *I've seen that one before.* I vividly remembered page 67 in my book depicting the vast vessel. But that was in the 12th century B.C. *No, it can't be.* Something lightly wiggled in my pocket. I felt around in search of the culprit. But, where my suit should have been, was a white dress that reached my ankles, which were laced with brown gladiator sandals.

The rustle in my dress pocket became louder, like crumpling paper. My leg was also freezing! I felt like my whole body was at the beach while my right leg was skiing in Colorado. I reached in and pulled out a folded piece of paper. Icicles clung to its edges, yet the paper was still intact. *Weird.*

What color was Helen's hair?

Those were the only words written on the whole sheet. *What is happening? Wait...*

"I'm in the Trojan War!" I shrieked out loud as I jumped up and down. Those were Achaean shacks! And that's the Wall of Troy! *This was amazing.* In all of the time travel movies I'd watched, the characters were scared, but I thought this was great! I started running through all of the people I might see: Helen of Troy was said to be the most beautiful woman alive, Menelaus was her husband, Paris was the Trojan who kidnapped her, and Odysseus was the wisest man of them all!

Speaking of men, I don't see a single woman. Maybe I should find something to wear so I can blend in with everyone. This would have been the perfect time for Fairy Godmother Magissa to show up and provide me with a disguise, since she thought it would be enjoyable to send me here. I waited for a second, in case she came to her senses... she didn't. I guess I had to work a little harder.

I shuffled toward the nearest tent to avoid being seen by other soldiers headed in my direction. I opened the flap and there it was... a complete set of war gear! I excitedly ran over to it and was elated to find that everything I needed was there. A noise came from the corner, and I turned to see a soldier sleeping in his bunk.

He suddenly shifted from lying on one shoulder to the other. I held my breath, hoping his eyes would not pop open. I carefully grabbed his war gear and ran as fast as I could. I placed the shield over my head so no one would see my face.

"Slow down, soldier!" someone bellowed at me.

"Sorry," I responded in a deep voice, as I slowed to a speed walk.

I stopped when I reached the sand and donned my outfit. That's when I saw it... The Trojan Horse. It was a massive wooden horse, just like in the book. The men at the base of the horse looked like ants next to this beast. Suddenly, an ear-splitting noise came from somewhere in the camp.

"All leaders report to Agamemnon's tent immediately!" the voice boomed.

Several men appeared from their tents and headed toward the noise. Agamemnon was the leader of the Greek army. This meeting must be important. I crept behind the tent and found a crack in the bottom to look in through. I made sure to stay very still to avoid being caught by any roaming soldiers.

"All right, game plan. Odysseus, you're up," a man said.

Odysseus immediately stood up and traveled to the front of the room. "Thank you, Agamemnon. This war has gone on way too long. My son is ten years old and I haven't seen him since he was an infant. This plan will guarantee us a victory over the enemy. Menelaus receives Helen back from Paris, Agamemnon receives glory, and the rest of us get to return home."

The leaders grunted in assent.

I knew The Trojan War lasted for ten years which means this was the last year.

"I'm sure you all have noticed the horse outside by the shore."

Yeah, it's pretty hard to miss.

"Well, that is our gift. Sinon, stand," Odysseus ordered.

A man huddled in the corner of the tent stood up and walked toward the wise hero.

"As we all know by now, Sinon is a very talented liar," Odysseus stated while patting Sinon on the back.

A few chuckles escaped from the men. I guessed Sinon had built a reputation for himself.

"Sinon will lead the soldiers who are pushing the horse to the entrance of the city. I'll let him take over from here."

Sinon stepped to the middle of the room and let his head droop down. When he lifted it up, his facial expression had changed and he placed his hands on his cheeks. "The Greeks left me behind and said they were going to return home." He flailed his arms for emphasis. "I saw all of their ships depart from the shores with my own two eyes. The Greek army told me to deliver this horse as an apology for all of the pain they have caused."

A big smile appeared on Odysseus's face and I could see the excitement in his eyes. "I suspect they will wheel the horse into their walls and have a celebratory feast, after that tale," he chuckled.

"But why would we be returning home?" one of the other leaders inquired.

"Ah, we will all be sailing to a nearby island, which will be out of sight of our poor foes. In the night, we will return to Troy and destroy it!" Odysseus let out a laugh.

"How are we going to get in the city?" someone challenged. "We can't just walk in."

"A group of soldiers, including myself, will be hiding in the horse and will open the door for the rest of the soldiers," Odysseus answered. "Any other questions?"

"Who's going to decide who gets in the horse?" a leader grunted.

"Only our best men will be allowed."

A rustle sounded from my pocket. I hurriedly pulled the paper out before anyone else could hear the sound and my eyes returned to the question about Helen's hair. My gaze shot back to Odysseus. *Is this how I find Helen?*

"We board when the golden sun shines directly in our eyes," Odysseus declared. "Enough talk. We have work to do, men. Meeting adjourned."

The leaders filed out of the room and went their separate ways. An officer pulled Odysseus to the side. I tiptoed closer to the tent, so I was in earshot.

"What do you mean he lost his armor? We need him in the horse!" Odysseus spat out.

"He said he woke up from his nap and it had disappeared," the officer responded.

A shot of warmth traveled down my leg. It was all the confirmation I needed. I had to get in that horse! This was my chance... I mustered up all my courage and tapped Odysseus on his shoulder. My leg began to warm up, as if for moral support.

Odysseus slowly turned around.

"Hello Odysseus." I cleared my throat, attempting to deepen my rather high-pitched voice. "I am Aurelius, son of Malcomus... uh, at your service... sir. I wanted to ask if there is room in the horse for another soldier." My nerves were quickly taking over. I threw my hand up to my forehead in a salute.

Odysseus glared at me as if he could see straight through my lie.

Just then, I had an epiphany: Ithacans probably never used this salute. *Does he know that I'm an imposter?* Worried thoughts filled my brain and I stood waiting for a few seconds while his eyes seemed to search my soul.

"Repeat that movement, now!" he bellowed. My arm shot up and I stood, frozen in place. Nervous sweat trickled down my back as I shook with fear. *I never should have challenged Ms. Magissa.*

Suddenly, Odysseus began to laugh. "I like that!" he exclaimed, mimicking my movement. "See you soon, Aurelius. There's always room for a prepared soldier."

He and the officer walked off, and I felt as if a boulder had been lifted from my chest. *I just talked to the mastermind himself.* According to my book, Odysseus wouldn't make it home for another ten years. I could not even begin to fathom not having any contact with my family for twenty years. I really had to get home! I pulled the paper out of my pocket and stared at the writing again.

It flashed black and gold, like a flickering light switch. Somehow, this had to be the key.

Right before the sun set, we packed into the wooden horse. Luckily, I was near the side, so I could peep through a small hole in the wood. If you could call it luck... I was stuffed in a giant horse with ancient soldiers and weapons on all sides. I shifted my leg, accidentally bumping into a brawny soldier, who sighed with frustration. I tried the other leg and knocked into a skinny soldier on the other side. *This is going to be a long night.*

"All set!" Odysseus called to the soldiers outside the horse.

They closed the "door" and made sure it was sealed tight. I could feel us moving in the direction of the city. I could see the soldier beside me shaking. And even though I knew what the outcome would be, I was anxious too.

When we finally arrived at the city, Sinon went forward with the plan. From my little peephole, I watched his dramatic movements as he told the story. He took his sweet time explaining why a giant horse was outside Troy's walls. A wary guard walked the perimeter of the horse, a sneer on his pudgy face.

A knocking sound came from the entrance, and it took everything within me to refrain from screaming. *They found the door.* My whole body shook uncontrollably, making an obvious noise. The brawny soldier from earlier nudged me into silence.

"Is this hollow?" the guard asked, knocking on the bottom of the horse.

"Yes, it is," Sinon answered nonchalantly. There was no hint of fear in his loud voice. He really was a proficient liar.

The guard walked straight to where the sound was coming from: my peephole. He placed his weapon on the ground and took off his helmet before moving to place his eye in the hole.

"Cautus, you're just wasting time... Wheel it in," his fellow guard said. "I see nothing wrong with it."

"Ok, wheel it in," Cautus said reluctantly.

"And you, what is your name?" a third guard asked Sinon.

"Mendax," he answered without hesitation.

"Well, Mendax, you are a Trojan now!" the guard said excitedly. "Come feast with us!"

"Gladly, sir," Sinon answered.

With much difficulty, we were wheeled into the walls of Troy. I heard many voices coming closer to the horse, attempting to get a good view. Bells rang around the whole city. I assumed they were party bells because people started pouring out of their homes. Cheers filled the streets for hours. People partied all around us and rejoiced for their victory. Little did they know their city would be burned in a few hours. *Sometimes you have to look a gift horse in the mouth - literally, in this case.*

Suddenly a man shoved me out of the way to look through my peephole.

"Menelaus, stop that!" I heard Odysseus whisper from a few feet away.

Menelaus! He served as king of Sparta and was Agamemnon's brother. After he moved out of the way, I looked out of my peephole and instantly saw the culprit of his anguish—Helen! "The face that launched a thousand ships" was walking around the horse, in awe of its beauty. Menelaus had not seen his wife in ten years because she was stolen by Paris of Troy.

Today, historians continue to debate whether or not she was kidnapped. She is referred to today as Helen of Troy so maybe she did leave willingly. Either way, Menelaus was left by himself. Agamemnon, his brother, led an army in an attempt to get her back for his sullen brother. Ten years later, they were still trying. If Monerica ever needed me to assemble an army for her, I definitely would. That's how strong our bond is. Maybe I had more in common with these ancient people than I thought.

As Helen stepped into the light of a nearby torch, I took the opportunity to examine her. She seemed to have a yellow light following her wherever she went. Her features were not particularly special. I had always imagined her to have flowing blonde hair, pale skin, and encapsulating eyes...but she had none of the aforementioned qualities. *Wait... no blonde hair!* Her hair was auburn. She looked identical to Ms. Magissa's picture—almost as if she had had her pose. *No, that's not possible.*

"Ow!" I exclaimed as a burning pain shot through my leg. Even though it was dark in there, I could feel every eye was on me, just as they were in the classroom. Helen turned at the noise but, mixed with all of the partying going on around her, she walked away.

My leg was on fire. This must mean I had all of the information I needed! I was still shocked about Helen's hair. But I had to focus on my escape. Would the ride come to get me? Would I have to summon it? I contemplated these questions as the celebration outside continued.

Hours later the party finally died down. Through my peephole, I saw people sleeping peacefully everywhere. This might have been their first moment of peace since the Greek army arrived on their shores.

"It's time!" Odysseus loudly whispered.

The men opened the door quietly and we quickly jumped out of the horse. The bone cracks we all made could've woken up the whole city if they weren't in such a deep sleep. *Ah, personal space is a beautiful thing!*

"Four of you will go and unlock the doors. You, you, you, and... you, "Odysseus said, pointing at me and three other men.

This is my chance! With the combined strength of the three muscular soldiers... and me, we were able to open the door in no time. A crowd of Greek soldiers had already formed outside. I weaved through them and headed for a tree.

I plopped down by the root of the tree and caught my breath. Thankfully, no one noticed me. *Probably because they were too busy thinking about all of the gold they were about to get.* I felt guilty that I unlocked the doors that led to such a horrible slaughter. All of these innocent people have to be murdered for one person's mistake. The paper was bunching at my side and I was ready to leave this place. I was anxious to get back to my family again. I pulled out my paper, ready to answer the question.

What color was Helen's hair?

"I don't have a pen!" I shouted. My head fell back against the tree. *The tree!*

I broke off a twig and concocted some ink out of sand and water. It was faint, but still there was something. I wrote "auburn" in my nicest handwriting. I had barely finished the "n" when I began to alight. The invisible roller coaster sped through the sky. I looked down at the burning city and immediately looked away.

When I opened my eyes, I was right back in my seat in my history classroom. I looked around to see if anyone saw what just happened. I locked gazes with a boy sitting to my right. His big blue eyes looked very concerned as he stared back at me.

"Are you ok?" he whispered.

"...Yes," I responded slowly. *What did he see?*

"Are we chatting during class?" Ms. Magissa asked as she turned from the chalkboard. "Do you want another try at answering my question... Aurelius?"

I cocked my head, zeroing in on her good eye. "Why yes, Ms. Magissa, I would. Helen actually had auburn hair."

"Why do you think that is?" Ms. Magissa asked.

"I guess, since she was considered the "most beautiful woman in the world" people assume she had blonde hair because Eurocentric qualities are considered pretty. It's nice to know the truth!"

It seemed that only Ms. Magissa and the boy next to me could hear what I was saying. All of the other students were in some sort of daze.

"I guess my book wasn't totally true."

"Boiling hot, Aurelie. Funny thing about truth... sometimes it changes with who's telling it." She snapped her fingers and turned to the rest of the class. "Next question: Who discovered America?"

"Christopher Columbus," the same blue-eyed boy answered.

"Are you sure about that, Bryce?" Ms. Magissa asked.

Bryce nodded, looking very satisfied with himself.

Ms. Magissa's yellow teeth reappeared.

Until the lions have their own historians, the hunter will always be the hero of the tale.

Good luck, Bryce.

Acknowledgments

I wish to thank the following people who believed in me and my dream, who believed in Cinnamongirl, and helped develop a fantastic writing program for girls. First, Deborah Santana, who not only enlightened me on the publishing industry, but presented the idea to James Head, who at the time was the CEO of the East Bay Community Foundation. James promised he would give Cinnamongirl $10,000 and that he would speak to his colleagues at other foundations. Soon after, we received $10,000 from the San Francisco Foundation. Thank you to Anya Booker, a beautiful writer who captured the blueprint of the program on the Cinnamongirl website. I thank Mina Witteman who saw the website and stepped-up breathing life into the idea, by establishing a partnership with the Bay Area Book Festival and developing the writing program.

I thank all the Cinnamongirl instructors and coaches who signed up to work with our girls at a mere request. These amazing women did the heavy lifting. They gave their time and talent to help our girls get their stories and poems on paper. They gave them great ideas, kept them motivated and encouraged. Instructors Rena Barron, Paulette Boudreaux, Lisa Moore Ramée, Michelle

Mush Lee, Deborah Santana, Nikki Shannon Smith, Misa Sugiura, Arisa White, and Mina Witteman, and coaches Althea Anderson, R.C. Barnes, Adolpha Cole, Kimberly Freeman, Grace Gaskins, Shawnee Gibbs, Shawnelle Gibbs, Hope Jones, Sarah Moen, Adriana Morera, Kathleen Phu, Lauren Randolph, Nneka Samuel, Kelsey Scott, Kristie Valdez-G, and Rita Woods: you have changed our girls' lives and I am forever grateful for that.

And lastly, I thank our brilliant Cinnamongirls who gave so much of their time, creative juices, and continued their writing journey despite the grueling writing blocks and all the nuances that accompany writing. Our Writergirls worked for months writing and re-writing during a stressful year of Covid-19. They worked on this project under the worst circumstances like remote learning without the structure of school they were used to, while not always having a private space to work and not knowing if they would see loved ones die to Covid. I thank you beautiful, brilliant, and resilient Writergirls!

Renée Richard
Founder and CEO Cinnamongirl, Inc.

cinnamongirl

BAY AREA
BOOK
FESTIVAL

Author Biographies

Mackenzie Bell

Mackenzie Bell is sixteen years old and in eleventh grade. Her dream for her future is to go to college and find a job in the line of medicine or law.

Kaya Bullard

Kaya Bullard is twelve years old and in seventh grade. Her ultimate dream is to be an entrepreneur and to create jobs for people that need it while also allowing her to do something she loves and is passionate about. She also dreams of her business to be extremely successful and known all around the world!

Laila Butcher

Laila Butcher is eighteen years old and a college freshman. Her dream is to be the founder and CEO of her own nonprofit for children of incarcerated parents and foster youth. She wants to promote mental, emotional, physical, and spiritual healing.

Giselle Caban

Giselle Caban is a sixteen-year-old junior in high school. Her dream is to accomplish everything she wants to in life. She wants to publish stories, go to college, become a lawyer, and so much more.

Naujda Davis-Van Hook

Naujda Davos-Van Hook is a fourteen-year-old eight grader. Her ultimate dream is to be someone who people can trust and relate to.

Aisha Renée Diop

Renée Diop is seventeen years old and a senior in high school. The past year has been like a sci-fi movie for her, just living out the days, trapped in the four walls of her room to pass the time. Now that we're out, her dream is to live life as fully as possible, not wanting to waste another second in boredom, or despair. Every decision she makes will benefit her in the present, instead of anticipating what may or may not come. She hopes everyone can learn to enjoy the moment, rather than sacrifice it by being anxious over the future.

Rowan Feldman

Rowan Feldman is fourteen years old and currently in eighth grade. Rowan is adopted. Her dream is to write songs. She loves writing songs because she can relate to other people when she's writing them. Every time she listens to a song she can relate to a lot of the lyrics. It's something she truly loves to do, and something she would love to continue in the future.

Jennifer Leon

Jennifer Leon is a graduate from Berkeley High School and now a freshman at Humboldt State University. An animal lover, Jenny's dream is to become a zoologist. Jenny says: "I am now finally able to pursue my dream and make it a reality!"

Mariah McCoy

Mariah is a fifteen-year-old writer who is in her sophomore year of high school. Mariah's dream is to make a difference in the world. She strongly believes in the notion that learning about history can shape the future. By analyzing the decisions made by one's ancestors, Mariah believes society will continue to progress. By writing *The Magic of Magissa*, Mariah hopes readers will do their own research and form their own opinions. The key to a more perfect union, according to Mariah, is to be educated in the past and prepare for the future.

Erikah Sanders

Erikah Sanders is a thirteen-year-old eighth grader. She has so many dreams that it is hard to choose one, but Erikah is confident that whichever one (or all!) she will pursue is going to come true.

Chariot Waddell

Chariot Waddell is fifteen years old and resides in Phoenix, Arizona with her parents and three younger siblings. As a sophomore in high school some activities that Chariot is involved in include playing lacrosse for her school, being a representative for the Shelectricty Youth Leadership Council, being a member of the National Honors Society, is the co-fundraising director for her school chapter of the Black Student Union. In her free time Chariot loves to participate in activities with her family and friends, read, write stories, plays, and poetry, and draw cartoons, mold clay, and create abstract art. Chariot is passionate about uplifting the black community and one day aspires to use her God-given gifts and talents to impact the world but for now, she's living her life to the fullest and taking life one day at a time.

Clover Waddell

Clover Waddell is thirteen years old and lives in Arizona. She is in eighth grade. She has so many aspirations and goals in life it's hard for her to name just one. Her dream for herself is that she would like to become a doctor. She wants to help impact people's lives and change the world for the good. She wants her life to have a purpose and as a child of God, she wants to continue to flourish and live through His favor.

Alanna Williams

Alanna Williams is sixteen years old and a sophomore in high school. Her dream is to make the world a more accepting place for people with mental health issues, specifically those who struggle with anxiety and or social anxiety. She hopes that we can become a society that engages in open and honest conversations that help to de-stigmatize what people think about mental health.

Jolie Wilson

Jolie Wilson is sixteen years old and a junior in high school. Jolie's dream is to become either a forensic psychologist or forensic pathologist. She's very hardworking and outgoing and what makes her stand out most is her creativity and choice to stand out from others.

Cinnamongirl Cohorts

Travelgirl
For girls poised to transform the world, Cinnamongirl designs life-altering travel experiences that are more than mere sight-seeing and cultural exchange. Our Travelgirls are encouraged to overcome limiting beliefs, recognize misguided perceptions, and embrace informed global citizenship.

This is a competitive cohort, hence the majority of our girls are selected from within the organization only after participating in at least one of our other cohorts. Girls ages 14-18.

Write Your Story
Girls who enjoy storytelling and writing participate in fantastic master classes led by critically acclaimed female writers.

Equipped with writing coaches and a supportive space, girls ignite life-long friendships, build their confidence, and hone their craft. This work culminates in a compelling anthology of stories and poetry professionally edited, bound and presented at the Bay Area Book Festival and other festivals. Girls ages 12-18.

Passport Book Club
Brilliant and curious book-loving tween girls come together to select, read and discuss books from around the globe. With bold female characters of color and written by women of color, our girls engage over rich remarkable stories typically not available in their schools.

Our achievers critically think, develop their voice, and expand their ideas. They participate in various podcasts and book talks. Girls ages 9-13.

Entrepreneurgirl
Our cohort of achievers embark on an entrepreneurial journey of master classes with accomplished women entrepreneurs who share their stories while discussing key elements of problem-solving, being your own boss, and how to bring your product to the market.

Our achievers leave the program with a fully developed pitch deck and a solid understanding of what it takes to be an Entrepreneur. Girls ages 12-18.

Cinnamongirl Inc.
We believe that when you immerse a girl in a powerful network, and provide her with amazing experiences, not only will she thrive, she will bring others along with her. Our phenomenal cohorts are where it all begins.

Ready to join our family?
Please visit https://www.cinnamongirl.org/